Lighthouses FOR KiDS

History, Science, and Lore
with 21 Activities

KATHERINE L. HOUSE

CHICAGO
REVIEW
PRESS

Library of Congress Cataloging-in-Publication Data

House, Katherine L.

   Lighthouses for kids: history, science, and lore with 21 activities /
Katherine L. House. — 1st ed.

     p. cm.

  Includes bibliographical references and index.

  ISBN-13: 978-1-55652-720-3

  ISBN-10: 1-55652-720-9

  1. Lighthouses—Juvenile literature. I. Title.

VK1013.H68 2008

387.1'55—dc22

2007027093

For Jim, Jonathan, and Caroline.
I couldn't have done it without them.

"I'd Like to Be a Lighthouse" © 1926 by Doubleday, a division of Random
House, Inc., from *Taxis and Toadstools* by Rachel Field. Used by permission of
Random House Children's Books, a division of Random House, Inc.

Cover and interior design: Rattray Design

Cover photos: Kid in front of lighthouse © Donald Nausbaum; all other
images, iStock.com

Published by Chicago Review Press, Incorporated

814 North Franklin Street

Chicago, Illinois 60610

ISBN 978-1-55652-720-3

Printed in the United States of America

5 4 3 2 1

Contents

Note to Readers

You might be surprised to find out that the word *lighthouse* means different things to different people. Lighthouse experts can't even agree on an exact definition. So what did I consider a lighthouse for this book? A structure designed to stand forever and provide a light to boaters. The structures highlighted in *Lighthouses for Kids* also featured an enclosed area (the lantern room) where the keeper could do his or her job. In nearly every case, a keeper lived at the lighthouse at some point in the past to tend the light. Finally, I chose to emphasize the lives of keepers and their families who were civilian workers, rather than more recent members of the U.S. Coast Guard.

Acknowledgments

Many people have played a role in helping me get this book published. Thanks to Jim and Barbara Leupold for introducing me to the magic of lighthouses as a child, and to my husband, Jim, who has grown to admire lighthouses almost as much as I do. My son, Jonathan, enthusiastically explained lighthouse technology to his friends and mastered the art of refracting light. My daughter, Caroline, patiently waited to discover mobility until this project was nearly finished. Maxine House read the manuscript with the keen eye of a retired English teacher.

Warm thanks to Jeremy D'Entremont, author of several lighthouse books and web-master of http://lighthouse.cc, who reviewed the entire manuscript. I appreciate his expertise, helpful comments, and attention to detail. I am also grateful to Millie Frese, who cheerfully read early drafts and offered so many suggestions. Thanks to SCBWI-Iowa for connecting me with the folks at Chicago Review Press, and to Lisa Rosenthal for her enthusiasm for the project. Cynthia Sherry helped me shape the manuscript into its current format, for which I am grateful. Lisa Reardon's careful and gentle guidance helped me through the final phases of the project.

Rebekah Frese and Amelia Moser read various chapters and tested activities. Thanks also to Alex Bussan, Beth Homan, and the Storey family for their suggestions.

Numerous friends cheered me on, including Cindy Blobaum, whose last-minute advice kept me going, Tess Judge-Ellis, who offered much encouragement during the journey to publication, and Claudia McGehee, sponge painter extraordinaire, who always asked good questions.

Special thanks to all the librarians, lighthouse experts, and local historians who provided research materials, photographs, and feedback; this project would not have been possible without them. The staff of the U.S. Coast Guard Historian's Office, especially Christopher Havern, was extremely helpful in providing access to their extensive collection. Finally, I appreciate the efforts of lighthouse keepers' families, who dug through photo collections to provide images for this book. Thanks to all!

Time Line

About 280 B.C.	The world's first lighthouse, Pharos, completed
About A.D. 50	Romans complete harbor at Ostia, including lighthouse
869	Lighted pagoda helps mark entrance to harbor in Shanghai, China
1157	Italians build lighthouse at Meloria
1669	Reflectors used in Swedish lighthouse
1698	First tower at Eddystone in England lighted
1699	Eddystone tower rebuilt and improved
1708	Third lighthouse at Eddystone lighted
1716	Lighthouse in Boston Harbor lighted
1719	First fog signal in colonial America used at Boston Harbor

1731	World's first lightship put in service in England
1759	Smeaton's Eddystone tower lighted
1769	First twin lights in United States established at Plymouth, Massachusetts
1781	First flashing light in a lighthouse installed in Sweden
	Aimé Argand develops new type of oil lamp about this time
1788	First range lights in United States built at Plum Island, Massachusetts
1789	Ninth Act of Congress puts federal government in charge of lighthouses
1792	Lighthouse at Cape Henry, Virginia, begins operating

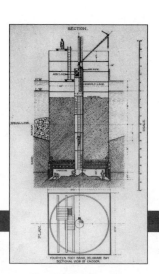

1798 Highland Light (Massachusetts) is first flashing light in United States	**1854** First lighthouse on West Coast starts operating on Alcatraz Island (California)
1812 Winslow Lewis sells U.S. government patent for oil lamps	**1855** Construction begins on second lighthouse at Minot's Ledge
1818 First lighthouse on Great Lakes completed at Buffalo, New York	**1869** First steam-powered fog signals used in United States
1820 First use of fog bell in United States	**1877** U.S. lighthouses begin to use kerosene
Stephen Pleasonton takes charge of U.S. lighthouses	**1882** Smeaton's Eddystone tower replaced
First lightship in United States in service on Chesapeake Bay	**1887** First pneumatic caisson lighthouse in United States built
1822 Augustin Fresnel invents Fresnel lens	**1907** Gustaf Dalén invents sun valve
1841 First Fresnel lens installed in United States at Navesink, New Jersey	**1910** Lighthouse Board dissolved; U.S. Bureau of Lighthouses (known as the Lighthouse Service) formed
1848 First screw pile lighthouse in United States built in Delaware Bay	**1939** U.S. Lighthouse Service merges with Coast Guard
1851 First Minot's Ledge Lighthouse in Massachusetts collapses	**1968** Coast Guard starts Lighthouse Automation and Modernization Program (LAMP)
Congress appoints commission to study state of lighthouses	**1983** Last U.S. lightship removed from service
1852 Stephen Pleasonton loses job; Lighthouse Board takes over	**2000** National Historic Lighthouse Preservation Act passed
	2005 Hurricane Katrina destroys three lighthouses; damages others

Introduction

Have you ever seen a lighthouse? If you live along a major coastline or have traveled near water, there's a good chance that you have. You might have spotted a lighthouse while walking along a beach, fishing, or sailing. Perhaps you have visited a museum about lighthouses or climbed to the top of an old lighthouse tower. Even if you have never seen a lighthouse up close, you have a good idea what one looks like. Pictures of lighthouses adorn the covers of books, magazines, greeting cards—even the bags of one brand of potato chips. Lighthouses flash at us from movies and TV ads.

Long before lighthouses were part of summer vacations or company advertising, they were essential parts of the landscape. At a time when rivers and oceans were the nation's highways, lighthouses served as warning signs, traffic lights, and maps, all rolled into one. Without lighthouses, it was harder for ships to get from one port to another safely. Without ships, it was difficult or impossible to send goods from one part of the country to another or obtain them from other nations. Without trade, people could not earn a living. In fact, the very growth and survival of the United States depended on a large network of reliable lighthouses.

The concept of a lighthouse seems simple now: shine a light from a building tall enough to be visible far away. As you will find out soon, accomplishing this was easier said than done. Today, when skyscrapers in the smallest cities dwarf the tallest lighthouses, it may be difficult to think of a lighthouse as an engineering marvel. But how could workers construct tall, sturdy buildings without concrete, steel, or modern machines? In this book you will learn about the daring builders and engineers who built lighthouses in places some said it was impossible to do so. You will learn how lighthouse designs and building methods were adapted to different locations.

At a time when you can order virtually anything you want and have it delivered overnight, it may seem hard to believe that getting building materials to a lighthouse site or supplies to a lighthouse could be time-consuming and dangerous. But how long would it take you to walk to the next town or row a boat three miles along a nearby river? *Lighthouses for Kids* includes firsthand accounts of the challenges of living and working in remote places, far from stores, schools, or doctors.

Nowadays, few people think about the everyday act of flipping light switches on and off. Even when the electricity goes out in your area, you have strong flashlights and perhaps generators to help you see. But how did people make lights at the top of a lighthouse tower powerful when they had only candles and oil lamps? In *Lighthouses for Kids*, you will learn about the Thomas Edison of lighthouses, a French scientist who revolutionized the way lighthouses worked. You will also discover the heroic efforts made by keepers simply to keep a light on all night.

As you make your way through this book, you will do more than read dramatic stories about the people who designed, built, and worked at lighthouses. Activities throughout the book will let you learn more about a keeper's daily life, from tending an oil lamp (with adult supervision) to polishing brass. You can use your imagination to write in a replica logbook as you wear an authentic-looking keeper's cap. You can experience life as a keeper's kid by planting a garden in sand or gravel, or by constructing a wind sock (there were lots of windy days at lighthouses). Through a series of science experiments, you will discover the challenges scientists and engineers faced when designing and building lighthouses. No matter what your interests, *Lighthouses for Kids* will shine new light on the work of keeping ships and sailors safe before modern technology made the job easier.

Chapter One

Growing Up at a Lighthouse
True Stories of Keepers' Kids

Eight-year-old Philmore Wass searched the shoreline as he scurried to the outhouse on a cold December morning in 1925. Low-lying fog on Maine's Libby Island kept him from seeing far. He could barely make out the shape of tall stakes that looked like fence posts sticking out of the water.

Puzzled, he ran back to the house and grabbed the spyglass that hung over the kitchen table. The magnifier revealed what his eyes could not see: the broken masts of a sailing ship. The ship must have wrecked the previous night when howling winds had kept him awake.

Philmore had seen shipwrecks before near this island where his father was a lighthouse keeper. Right now, Dad was on the mainland with Philmore's older brother. Mrs. Wass called the nearby Coast Guard station to tell them about the tragedy. The Wass family was lucky to have a telephone. Not all homes—and certainly not all lighthouses—had one in the 1920s. The Wass's phone worked using an underground cable that often went out in bad storms. On this day, it was working, and Philmore's mother was relieved to learn that the ship's crew had been rescued.

The lighthouse keeper's son could not wait for the fog to lift so that he could see what had happened. How big was the ship? What cargo had it been carrying? What kind of damage had it endured? Philmore remembered an earlier shipwreck near rocky Libby Island. He had been sad to see a majestic ship destroyed by the unpredictable force of the sea. After the fog lifted, Philmore realized the ship must have been heading to one of New England's many paper mills. Cords of wood floated on the water, turning it a whitish-brown color.

Inset: Young Philmore Wass, shown here when he was eight years old, moved to Maine's Libby Island in 1919 when he was two years old. His father was the head keeper of the Libby Island Lighthouse. *Courtesy of Philmore B. Wass*

Maine's Libby Island Lighthouse. *U.S. Coast Guard Historian's Office*

Philmore, his sister Nonie, and her friend went outside to explore. They walked the length of snow-covered Libby Island to reach the sandbar separating it from its neighboring island, "Big Libby." As they drew closer, they noticed that two of the ship's three masts were still connected to the deck, but leaned at an odd angle. The rigging, or ropes that supported the sails, swung back and forth in the wind. The ship's shredded sails hung from cords of wood. "It was difficult to comprehend that the wind and the seas, combined with the destructive power of Libby's Ledges, could so totally destroy a ship of this size and strength in a few hours," he wrote.

When the tide went out, the children waded across the bar to the wreck. "Feeling like midgets, we stood near the hull and looked up at the largest man-made structure we had ever seen," Philmore recalled. The three managed to reach the stern, or rear, of the *John C. Myers* and climb aboard. Dishes, food, even furniture, had been hurled about. The odor of large chunks of salt pork floating in the water made Philmore's stomach flip-flop. Like others who lived along the coast at the time, the keeper's son knew that once a ship was totally wrecked, anyone could salvage what was left. The search for souvenirs began.

Soon he spotted a beautiful black mahogany box. Hoping that it held treas-

ures, Philmore opened it. It was empty, except for its lovely velvet lining. Philmore wondered if the box had held a sextant or maybe a compass to help the captain find his way. Had the crew rescued the valuable instrument, or was it lost forever in the cold dark ocean? The children could not linger long. If the tide came in, they would be trapped for hours on "Big Libby." Armed with his precious box, Philmore began to walk home with the older girls. "It had been a unique and exciting adventure," he realized. "How many other kids ever had a chance to explore a wrecked ship hours after she had struck the rocks?"

Besides having the rare chance to explore shipwrecks, children of lighthouse keepers peered into tide pools, scoured the shoreline for treasures, and learned to handle boats at an early age. Often their brothers and sisters were the only children to play with. Sometimes it was difficult to keep quiet so that the tired keepers could catch up on sleep during the day. From the time they were young, lighthouse children helped with chores to keep the lighthouse and the keeper's house clean and orderly. Most important, they were proud of the jobs their fathers and mothers held. Even in times of illness, bad weather, and family crisis, they did what they could to keep the lights burning.

Decorate a Seashell Picture Frame

When their family lived at San Diego's Old Point Loma Lighthouse, Henry, Robert, and Joseph Israel liked to collect shells from the nearby beach. Their father, Robert Sr., was lighthouse keeper there from 1871 to 1891. Their mother, Maria, was an assistant keeper from 1873 to 1876. The boys polished the shells with a grindstone and sold them to visiting tourists. They also gave smaller shells to their mother, who made decorative frames to sell. You can use shells to decorate a frame, too.

If you want the same type of shell in each corner or along each edge, set four similar shells aside. Place the remaining shells in a second pile and broken pieces in a third one.

Use the craft stick to spread glue along one edge of the frame within the marked-off area. Press each shell firmly into the glue. Apply more glue as needed. Fill in the spaces between the shells with broken pieces. Let each side dry before tackling another side. Insert a picture when all the glue has dried.

You'll Need

Old newspapers
Ruler
Pencil
Clear plastic 5 × 7-inch (12.7 × 17.8-cm) picture frame that stands up by itself (horizontal or vertical)
Small decorative shells (sold in craft stores)
Craft stick
Clear tacky craft glue

Cover work surface with newspapers. Use your ruler and press firmly with your pencil to mark off a 1-inch (2.5-cm) border around every side of the frame.

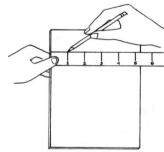

NO FAMILIES ALLOWED

At very isolated and dangerous lighthouses, families were not allowed to live with keepers. Lighthouses where only male keepers lived were called "stag stations." Lighthouses in Alaska and some off-shore lighthouses in other states were stag stations. In some cases, the government permitted the keeper's family to visit for short periods.

Treasures from the Sea

Whether they lived on an island or on the mainland, along the ocean, a lake, or a river, children who grew up at lighthouses looked for adventure along the water. They often walked the coastline in search of shells, driftwood, or other treasures. For some, a new tide might even bring exotic food.

William Spear Jr. grew up along the Delaware Bay where his father served as keeper of the Deepwater Range Lights for over 30 years. After a shipwreck, bunches of canned food floated ashore, but not before their labels washed off. "Mother would open a can, hoping that it would be beans or tomatoes, and we would be delighted to find out that it contained peaches or cherries," he later recalled.

Not every shipwreck brought such a selection of treats. Harold Jennings was born in 1921 on an island in Boston Harbor, where his father was a lighthouse keeper. Once, after a ship wrecked nearby, 150-pound (68 kg) boxes of coconut washed ashore. "I thought I would never want to see another shred of coconut in my life," Harold later wrote. "We would have coconut in everything."

More often, the sea provided daily food and sometimes treats. In southern California, Norma Engel often pried abalone, a type of mollusk, off the rocks at low tide. Her father was a keeper at Ballast Point Lighthouse in the early 1900s. Sometimes the family dried the "meat" from the shells on the fence. "It was cheaper than gum, there was always a ready supply, it satisfied our hunger for a spell, and it was an excellent gum massage," Norma remembers.

Water and Gardens

Finding fresh seafood was not usually a problem for keepers' families; having enough water to drink was. In some places, keepers had access to springs or wells. Families living along freshwater lakes drank lake water. Salt water could not be used for drinking water, so many lighthouse families relied on water collection systems. When it rained, water was funneled off the keeper's house into a large container called a cistern. Sometimes bird droppings or dirt from the roof made its way into the water. In dry regions, keepers constantly worried about having enough to drink.

Harold Jennings, 1929.
Scituate Historical Society Archives

4

Keeping a Garden: Was It Possible?

Differing water and terrain conditions made it easier to grow plants at some lighthouses than at others. This experiment will let you grow plants in conditions similar to those at different lighthouses.

You'll Need

Old newspapers
Ballpoint pen
4 20-oz. (0.6-L) Styrofoam
    coffee cups
Tape measure
Plastic spoon
Potting soil, sand, and gravel
Four bean or pea seeds
Disposable plastic container for
    mixing dirt
Plastic trays to catch water (lids
    from take-out containers or
    plastic picnic plates)
Liquid measuring cup (for water-
    ing plants)

Place newspapers on work surface, or work outside. Use the pen to number the cups: 1, 2, 3, 4. Use your tape measure to mark a place on the exterior of each cup 2 inches (5 cm) from the bottom and 4 inches (10 cm) from the bottom. Use your hands or the spoon to fill Cup 1 evenly with 2 inches (5 cm) of soil, using the mark on the outside as a guide. Position a seed in the cup's center; cover with 2 more inches (5 cm) of soil. In Cup 2, plant a seed in sand the same way. In Cup 3, plant a seed in gravel using the same method. Fill the bottom 2 inches (5 cm) of Cup 4 with sand; add soil up to the 4-inch (10-cm) mark. Pour cup contents into container

and mix with spoon. When well mixed, place 2 inches (5 cm) of the soil/sand back in Cup 4. Plant a seed; cover with remaining mixture.

While holding cups over the plastic tray, use your pen to poke four holes in the bottom of each one. (Be careful; some sand will fall out.) Nourish each seed with about 2 ounces of water; dump the excess liquid off tray into sink. Place the trays near a sunny window. When watering, use the same amount of liquid for each seed. Do you think all the seeds will grow? Why? Why do you think keepers on a rocky Maine island hauled dirt to their island every spring?

The keepers at Scotch Cap Lighthouse in Alaska pose with a Christmas tree. No trees grew on the island; a passing ship delivered the tree to the keepers. *U.S. Coast Guard Historian's Office*

Taking care of a vegetable or flower garden was a common pastime for lighthouse keepers and their families. Fresh vegetables were a nice treat at stations far from stores, and growing food saved keepers money. Flower gardens cheered families in areas used to fog or bleak winters. Working in a garden was also a good way to pass time.

Dangers All Around

Lighthouse children learned from an early age that their rugged surroundings could be dangerous. High winds could suddenly capsize a small boat. A wave that did not look very big could come ashore with such force that it could hurl objects—and even people—into the sea. Without knowledge of tidal patterns, someone could become stranded on a low-lying piece of land or have trouble maneuvering a boat.

To ensure the safety of young children, parents sometimes used ropes to make a harness or leash. Naturally, the rope was short enough that a child could not reach the water or fall over a cliff. On Petit Manan Island off the coast of Maine, the keeper and his wife beckoned children back to the house with a bell if they thought their offspring had wandered too far.

The steep clay cliffs surrounding the Point Arena Lighthouse in California presented constant problems. The Owens family moved to the light station in 1937, and six Owens sisters called the light station home. One day, three of the girls used a ladder to get down the cliffs so that they could play in a cave. Unfortunately, while they were playing, the tide came in, and they could no longer get to the ladder. The oldest girl managed to scale the cliff,

Cliffs surrounding California's Point Arena Lighthouse, shown here in 1934, made the area dangerous for both children and animals. *U.S. Coast Guard Historian's Office*

SURPRISE! WHEN UNEXPECTED VISITORS ARRIVE

Rebecca and Abigail Bates must have been uneasy. It was September 1814, and the United States was at war with Great Britain. The young women lived with their family at the Scituate Lighthouse in Massachusetts, where their father was keeper. One day when their father was away, a British warship appeared off the coast. Rebecca and Abigail watched as soldiers climbed into smaller boats to row ashore. Would they attack the lighthouse? What would happen to their town?

The Bates sisters knew they needed to do something—and do it fast. Hidden from view, Rebecca began playing a drum belonging to a local soldier. Her sister grabbed a fife. When the ship's commander heard the music, he mistook it for enemy soldiers. Worried about his men, he ordered them to return to the man-o'-war. The sisters are known in Scituate as "The American Army of Two." To this day, they get credit for saving the town, although details of what happened are sketchy.

The story of the Bates girls illustrates the dangers of living at an isolated lighthouse. Keepers and their families sometimes had to contend with enemy soldiers, criminals, and other unwelcome guests. In 1927, a 12-year-old girl named Betty Byrnes tried to scare away criminals near the Point Iroquois Lighthouse in northern Michigan near the border with Canada. Her father was keeper there during Prohibition, a time when it was illegal to possess beer, wine, or liquor. Betty and her siblings knew that smugglers liked to haul the banned beverages across a nearby river separating the United States and Canada. They had discovered hidden cases of banned drinks. At night, they heard boats and saw cars flash headlights across the river as a secret code.

Betty knew anyone who caught "rum runners" earned a reward. "We dreamed of having enough money to order anything we wanted from the Sears Roebuck Catalog,"

Betty Brynes once tried to catch smugglers near the Point Iroquois Lighthouse in northern Michigan.
U.S. Forest Service

she recalled. One night, Betty slipped away with two brothers and a sister. One of her brothers carried an unloaded gun; Betty wore her father's old sheriff's badge. They planned to stop the smugglers' car with a rope tied to trees on either side of a nearby road. They waited and waited.

When a speeding car came along, the vehicle snapped the rope, nearly uprooting the small trees. Disappointed, the Byrnes children began to walk home. Their father met them partway and demanded to know what was going on. "We started crying and the whole story came out," Betty recalled. "He was furious! He told us that these men were armed and dangerous. We could have been killed. . . . We were in the doghouse for days and had many privileges taken away." Even so, Betty often wondered what would have happened if the rope had been stronger.

but her younger sisters could not. The oldest sister retrieved ropes from the fog signal building and somehow managed to haul her siblings up the cliff. Their parents did not find out about the incident until the girls told them many years later.

The terrain posed hazards for animals, too. The family cow once made it to a ledge several feet below the lighthouse, but she could not get back up. To rescue Bessie, Keeper Owens had to tie one end of a rope to a car and the other end around the cow. As the vehicle was driven away from the cliff, Bessie gradually rose up over the bluff, thanks to the pushing and prodding of some men who had gone to the ledge to help.

Jean, Diana, and Joan Owens at the Point Arena Lighthouse with their dog, Pal. *The Owens family*

Bessie was fine, but the family dog, Pal, was not as lucky. After he fell to the beach below the lighthouse, he died from injuries a few days later.

Even though families were careful, the threat of drowning was a constant danger. Sometimes a curious child got too close to slippery rocks or did not pay attention to nearby waves. On a hot day, the water might have been too tempting for a child, even one who could not swim. Over time, several keepers' children drowned while playing near the water, or traveling back and forth to an offshore lighthouse. The heart-wrenching possibility of having a child drown was not the only thing that worried keepers. Families living at offshore stations could not get to town when the seas were rough, causing Mrs. Wass "an ever-present fear that [a family member] might sustain a serious injury."

Because of this isolation, keepers learned to be resourceful when it came to medical care, just as they were used to fixing things at the lighthouse. Vernon Gaskill and his siblings liked to run up and down the stairs of the Cape Hatteras Lighthouse for fun. Their father was a keeper at the North Carolina lighthouse. One day, Vernon's younger brother fell down the stairs and bit his tongue, leaving a little piece barely hanging on. "Daddy took the scissors that he used to trim the [wick] and cut it off," remembers Vernon. "It didn't affect his speech any but he had a little less tongue than he had before."

Playing Around

In the summer, when it was warm and storms were less frequent, lighthouse children took advantage of opportunities their lifestyle offered. In places with a sandy shoreline, they swam in the nearby lake or ocean. On a rocky island, they might transform a large tide pool into a swimming hole. Picnics at a scenic spot near the water were a favorite activity, especially on Sundays. Depending on where they lived and weather conditions, lighthouse children sometimes used a small boat. First, though, they had to be old enough and strong enough to handle the boat's oars.

Keepers' kids also had to learn to tie knots to secure their boat wherever they went. When the family of Keeper Roscoe Chandler of Maine's Blue Hill Bay Lighthouse went on a picnic on a nearby island, one of the children failed to secure the boat properly, and it floated away. Quick thinking to the rescue! The keeper and the children gathered driftwood while Mrs. Chandler tore her petticoat into strips. After assembling a raft from these supplies, the keeper paddled out to the boat. The children probably received a knot-tying lesson after that!

Libby Island lighthouse keepers and their families pose for a photo on the Maine island. Philmore Wass is pictured on the left, bottom row, standing beside his older sister Winona ("Nonie"). Their brother Irwin is second from the right, bottom row. *Courtesy of Philmore B. Wass*

This photo of the Ballast Point Lighthouse and the keeper's family was taken before the Engel family lived there. The lighthouse no longer stands. *U.S. Coast Guard Historian's Office*

Tie a Bowline Knot

With practice and patience, you can learn to tie knots. The bowline (pronounced bow-lin) is a good, all-purpose knot used for creating a secure loop. People use it when camping, sailing, and mountain climbing. It is also a good knot for rescuers.

You'll Need

3 feet (1 m) of rope, any type

Hold the rope by placing one hand on one end (the leading end) and the other hand at about the halfway point. Take the leading end and loop it under the rope to form a sideways number "6."

Holding the loop in place with one hand, use your other hand to stick the trailing piece up through the center of the loop.

Weave the long trailing end under the short leading end at the top of the "6," then insert the trailing end back down through the top of the loop in the "6."

Here comes the tricky part: tightening the knot without losing your loop. Grab each end of the rope with one hand and pull as hard as you can.

"Use of the rowboat opened a new world for me," according to Norma Engel. "It was my magic carpet (not without some effort on my part), taking me wherever I wished, floating up the bay, across to the fort wharves for play with other children, drifting out to the open ocean, or seeking out the best places for good fishing. My magic carpet carried me to the limits of my strength and endurance."

Knowing how to watch for signs in the sky and water of changing weather was essential for anyone who lived along the water. Before the Weather Channel, radio, or the Internet, people had to develop their own weather forecasts. On White Island, New Hampshire, where Celia Thaxter's father was a lighthouse keeper, Celia and her brother watched a small plant for clues about the weather. The scarlet pimpernel "clasped its small red petals together, folding its golden heart in safety from the shower that was sure to come," Celia later wrote. Another keeper's child recalled, "You get in touch with nature, and so much of your life hinges on knowing what's going to happen with the weather. You get to a point where you know when it's going to rain or the fog is coming."

Growing up in such isolated areas, kids had to be creative when they played. "Kites became a blessing to us," recalls Glenn

Dealing with Isolation

Lighthouse life was not for everybody. While Philmore Wass enjoyed his childhood on a Maine island as the son of a lighthouse keeper, his sister said she "hated the place." Many children lived too far from towns to participate in scouting, clubs, or church activities. Depending on the location of the lighthouse, there might be only a few other children around, living at a nearby fishing village, life-saving station, or military fort. At light stations with more than one keeper, children often had other children to socialize with. In other cases, lighthouse children had only brothers and sisters to play with.

Annie Bell Hobbs lived on Boon Island in the late 19th century. Her father was a lighthouse keeper on the island nine miles (14.5 km) offshore in the Atlantic Ocean. No trees, shrubs, or even grass grew on the rocky island. Besides teenaged Annie, only two younger children called Boon Island home: her three-year-old brother and the four-year-old daughter of another keeper. In 1876, when Annie was about 14, she wrote an article for a children's magazine in which she said she had been "a prisoner" on Boon Island for two years. She reflected on her lonely life, "After school-hours, I turn my eyes and thoughts toward the mainland and think how I should like to be there, and enjoy some of those delightful sleigh-rides

Glenn Furst loved to make miniature sailboats while growing up at the North Manitou Island Lighthouse in Michigan. The lighthouse no longer stands. *U.S. Coast Guard Historian's Office*

Furst, who grew up on North Manitou Island, Michigan, where his stepfather was a keeper. "When we didn't know what to do, we would make a kite." Glenn and his younger brother also liked to collect small pieces of driftwood. They pierced the wood with a nail to make a hole for a seagull feather sail. As soon as their miniature sailboats floated out into the lake, the boys

attacked them with rocks, pretending the boats were enemy warships.

At the Matinicus Island Light Station in Maine, two boys created a miniature fishing village on a pond, complete with small houses, wharves, toy boats, and a lighthouse.

Make a Lighthouse Wind Sock

Children living at lighthouses liked to make their own kites and fly them for amusement. It was often breezy along the water, and at many lighthouses, there were few things for kites to become tangled on. In the spirit of kite building, you can build a wind sock shaped like a lighthouse in this advanced activity.

Adult supervision required

You'll Need

Old newspapers
3 5-inch (12.7-cm) diameter cheap wooden embroidery hoops
Masking tape
Pencil
Measuring stick
2 10-inch (25.4-cm) pieces of ¼ × ¹⁄₁₆-inch (.64 × .016-cm) spruce wood (from a hobby store)
Glue gun
3 clothespins with spring hinges
10 × 17-inch (25.4 × 43.2-cm) piece of white ripstop nylon for the lighthouse tower
Permanent markers
2 3-inch (7.6-cm) diameter cheap wooden embroidery hoops
2 3-inch (7.6-cm) pieces of ¼ × ¹⁄₁₆-inch (.64 cm × .016-cm) spruce wood

2 10-inch (25.4-cm) pieces of sturdy wire
3 × 11-inch (7.6 × 27.9-cm) piece of yellow ripstop nylon for the light-house light
6 1 × 12-inch (2.5 × 30.5-cm) pieces of yellow ripstop nylon
Paper hole punch
3 feet (1 m) sturdy string or twine

Your wind sock will have two sections: the tower and the lantern room.

To make the tower section:
Unscrew the 5-inch (12.7-cm) embroidery hoop fasteners and remove inner hoops; discard outer hoops. Stack the inner hoops on top of each other; fasten with tape. Turn stack on side and use the measuring stick to mark a straight line inside the hoops. Roll the stack halfway around, make a similar mark and remove tape.

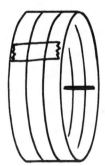

Lay the 10-inch (25.4-cm) pieces of spruce wood flat. Use your measuring stick to mark a line 1 inch from either end and one in the center of both pieces.

Use the glue gun to apply a few drops of glue just to the right of the first mark on one piece of spruce wood. Press one hoop into the glue, lining up the left edge of the hoop with the mark on the spruce wood. Align the mark inside the hoop along the top edge of the spruce wood. Clamp with a clothespin. Use the same method to glue remaining hoops to spruce wood at other two marks.

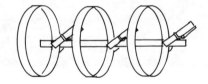

When dry, remove clothespins and roll the frame halfway around. Attach hoops to remaining 10-inch piece of wood, as above.

While your framework dries, use your pencil to draw a line ½-inch from each short (10-inch) side of the white nylon, which will form your tower. Use markers to add windows and a door, then add stripes or another pattern, if desired.

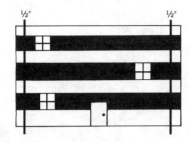

To make the lantern room section:
Unscrew the 3-inch (7.6-cm) embroidery hoop fasteners and remove inner hoops; discard outer hoops. Use the same method you used with the 5-inch hoops to make two marks on the insides of the 3-inch hoops.

Mark lines on the 3-inch pieces of spruce wood ½-inch (1.3-cm) from each end.

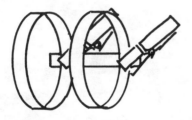

Attach the 3-inch hoops to the 3-inch pieces of spruce wood at both marks, as above.

When both frames dry, attach the 10-inch pieces of wire to the tower frame at the spots where the spruce wood supports and hoops join. To ensure a secure connection, twist the wire firmly against the wood.

To attach the white nylon tower to the 5-inch frame, place the top of the "tower" closest to the end with wires. With the frame lying on its side, apply glue to one piece of spruce wood and half of each hoop at the same time. Align the edge of the nylon with the edge of the spruce wood, then have one person roll the frame slowly, counterclockwise, as the other person presses the nylon into the glue. Attach the other half of the nylon to the frame by the same method. Finish the tower by adding glue to the underside of the loose flap of nylon. Press onto frame; let dry.

Twist the loose end of the wires around the 3-inch frame at the spots where the spruce wood supports join the hoops. Attach the 3 × 11-inch (7.6 × 28-cm) piece of nylon to the hoops the same way you attached the white nylon to the larger frame. This will be a bit more cumbersome since both frames are attached to each other.

For finishing touches, glue the 1 × 12-inch (2.5 × 30.5-cm) pieces of nylon at even intervals around the inside of the bottom embroidery hoop forming the lighthouse tower.

Make two holes in the yellow nylon by pressing firmly through the fabric with the hole punch. Stick string through the holes, and tie your wind sock securely to a hook outside or the branch of a tree.

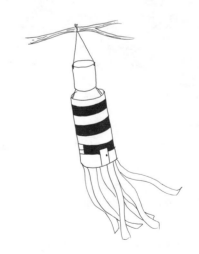

13

It is easy to see why Annie Bell Hobbs felt like a prisoner on Boon Island. *U.S. Coast Guard Historian's Office*

which I am deprived of while shut out here from the world."

When the weather was too stormy or cold to be outside, lighthouse families had to make the most of being stuck indoors. "I don't think there is any view that is any-more lonely and cold looking than a lake covered with ice," recalled Furst. On New Hampshire's White Island, it was so cold in the winter that frost accumulated on the inside of the windows in the keeper's house. For amusement, Celia Thaxter and her brother liked to press coins in the frost to create unusual patterns.

Families passed time inside playing cards, cribbage, dominos, and other games. About 1876, the Lighthouse Service began shipping portable libraries to the most isolated lighthouse stations. The libraries aimed to make the keepers "more contented with the lonely life and routine duties" of their jobs. About 40 books for adults and children were stored in a wooden carrying case. The invention of radio in the early 20th century improved life, too. Suddenly, keepers could receive current news, listen to church services, and hear weather forecasts and sports broadcasts. In some places, private citizens provided free radios to keepers to make their lives more interesting.

Going to School

The isolated lifestyle also made it challenging to get to school. Even for lighthouse families living on the mainland, school could be a few miles away. Before cars were invented, a two-mile (3-km) trip could be long and agonizing, especially in deep snow. Children living at offshore stations faced a bigger obstacle. They could go to school only when the weather was calm enough to launch a boat. If the weather worsened during the day, they had to spend the night with a friend or relative on the mainland. Sometimes parents served as teachers. Some families even sent their children to live with

A reproduction of a traveling library box, which was filled with books and sent to different lighthouses, is on display at Oregon's Heceta Head Lighthouse. *Ted Panayotoff*

someone on the mainland or requested a transfer to a mainland lighthouse when their children got older.

Harold Jennings was lucky. When his father was a keeper on an island in Boston Harbor, Harold often rode army boats that served the island to school. (Army caretakers watched over an old fort.) Sometimes he hitched a ride on the city's police boats and fireboats. Imagine Harold's surprise when the fireboat he was riding on one day was called to a fire at a nearby lighthouse! The

crew managed to rescue the keeper, but the structure was ruined.

Even well into the 20th century, getting to school could be tricky. In the late 1960s, Rickie Winchester and his sister lived at Cape Neddick Lighthouse near York, Maine. A narrow channel separated the lighthouse from the mainland. A previous keeper had strung up a large wooden box that glided along a cable over the channel. Mr. Winchester started using the box to transport his children to the mainland for

Glenn Furst, as a baby, with his brother, Norman, his sister, Ethel, and his father and mother. *Charles Furst*

Another year, Glenn's older sister taught school on the mainland. Glenn and his sister boarded with a family there, and his sister was his teacher!

In the early 20th century, the Lighthouse Service worked with some states and volunteer groups to help keepers' kids get an education. In a few cases, when kids could not get to school, schools came to them. Betty Byrnes remembers the small school that operated in an old storehouse at the Point Iroquois, Michigan, Lighthouse. The keepers remodeled the room, the state supplied blackboards, books, and desks, and the federal government provided a potbellied stove for heat. The state of Michigan paid the salary of a beginning teacher, and the Lighthouse Service paid her room and board. Six keepers' children attended, along with three from a fisherman's family.

In Maine in the early 1900s, the Maine Sea Coast Mission sent teachers to offshore light stations for about a month at a time. In such cases, the teachers lived in the keeper's house, along with their students! Mary Ellen Chase remembered teaching "in the rather bare room at the base of the light tower" in the 1920s. Chase later recalled that when she was not instructing the children, they were teaching her. She learned how to row a boat better, how to tie complex knots, and how to climb to the top of the lantern room without getting dizzy.

school. When word got out about this unusual method of transportation, the Coast Guard put an end to the practice. Officials said the box was unsafe for children.

Glenn Furst's family struggled more than most to find a suitable arrangement. One year, Glenn's older siblings walked four and a half miles (7 km) each way to an island school. Glenn traveled by horse and buggy to the island school one year, but only stayed until November. When the lake froze

and the lighthouse closed, the family moved to the mainland for the winter, and he switched schools.

When Glenn was in fifth grade or so, he and his younger brother George stayed with a couple on the mainland. "School went along pretty good but, of course, we were lonely and homesick, particularly at night," he recalled. When the lighthouse closed that winter, his family moved to a different town, and the kids switched schools again.

A Unique Childhood

Unlike children whose parents worked in a factory or office, children of lighthouse keepers could spend time with their families even while their parents were working. Mazie Freeman recalled that she always knew where to find her father on Petit Manan Island. "He may have been in the log room writing, in the whistle house painting, or on the shore picking up wayward lobster traps. When I needed his company, he was neither too far away, nor too busy to share a few moments with me."

Betty Byrnes summed up her childhood this way: "Children of the lighthouse keepers had a wonderful life. . . . We had boats to row, woods to roam, and our parents always at hand. I would not change my childhood as it was exciting, happy, and full of wonder."

VERY IMPORTANT VISITORS

Young Emmett DeRusha stood on the dock at Devils Island, Wisconsin, waiting for a special visitor. Emmett, who was about five years old, was dressed in new clothes his mother had sewn for the occasion and a new bow tie. It was August 1928. Emmett's family lived on the island where his father was an assistant keeper of the lighthouse.

Soon a yacht came into sight, escorted by a steamer, a Coast Guard boat, and two speedboats. After the yacht docked, Emmett and his family watched as President Calvin Coolidge and his wife got off the boat. Emmett bowed for the president and First Lady, who wore a plum-colored suit and white felt hat. His four sisters curtsied for the important visitors. About 50 people had come to the island for a picnic, includ-

ing Secret Service men, newspaper reporters, the president's doctor, and friends of the president and First Lady. The Coolidges were spending the summer nearby at a private home in northern Wisconsin.

After the picnic, the First Lady wiped chocolate cake off Emmett's face and re-tied a ribbon on his sister Edna's new dress. The president's party stayed about two hours before sailing off for another island. "The President and Mrs. Coolidge expressed themselves as well pleased with the visit and hoped they would be able to make another visit next year," the light keeper reported to his bosses. The *Lighthouse Service Bulletin* said, "It is believed that this is the first time in a long while that a station had been honored by a visit from the President."

FLYING SANTA DELIVERS CHRISTMAS CHEER

Seamond Ponsart could hardly wait to reach the package that had been dropped from an airplane. It was Christmastime 1945, and Seamond, who was five years old, lived at the Cuttyhunk, Massachusetts, lighthouse where her father was keeper. She knew the package was a gift from the "Flying Santa." Sadly, her bundle hit a rock, and the doll inside was crushed. Heartbroken, Seamond cried herself to sleep that night. Her mother wrote the Flying Santa, a man named Edward Rowe Snow, and told him what happened. Snow, a New England author, dropped care packages to lighthouse families each December containing small toys, candy, books, and magazines. He even included dog biscuits if he knew a dog lived at the light station.

Young Seamond Ponsart, her mother and father, and the "Flying Santa," 1946. *Dorothy Snow Bicknell Collection*

In 1946, the Ponsarts moved to the West Chop Lighthouse. Imagine Seamond's surprise that December when the Flying Santa arrived in a helicopter to deliver a package in person. "He landed at the Gay

Head Lifesaving Station [nearby] and there, like a fairy tale, I had Santa Claus hand me a doll to replace the broken one," she recalled as an adult.

The tradition of the Flying Santa started in 1929. Captain William Wincapaw, a Maine pilot, wanted to thank local lighthouse keepers for their work. Lighthouses had often helped him find his way home. Through the years, volunteers have kept the tradition going.

What happened to Seamond Ponsart? After she grew up, she served in the Coast Guard. In 2003 she flew in a helicopter with the modern-day Flying Santa. Seeing the joy on children's faces when the Flying Santa came to see them "was a top event of my lifetime," she says.

Chapter Two

Why Lighthouses?

A Short History

For much of history, ships hauled most goods from one region to another. Today, trucks, trains, and airplanes do that work. But when you order something online or from a catalog, you still pay "shipping" fees, a term left over from the days when nearly everything was hauled by boat. Rivers, canals, and lakes were the highways of long ago. Those routes did not have street signs or traffic lights to keep people safe. Instead, sailors came to rely on lighthouses to reach their destinations safely.

Ancient Lighthouses and Beyond

The oldest known lighthouse in the world was built over 2,000 years ago in ancient Egypt. It was called Pharos after the island where it was located. It is likely that ancient civilizations had used fires to aid sailors before this tower was built. There may even have been other lighthouses built earlier, but no records exist to tell us about them. For this reason, Pharos gets the credit as the world's first lighthouse.

The towering structure stood in the city of Alexandria, Egypt, at the point where the Nile River met the warm waters of the Mediterranean Sea. The island of Pharos, like much of the Nile Delta, was relatively flat, so people needed a way to raise up a fire to guide sailors. No one knows exactly what Pharos looked like or how tall it was, but it probably stood somewhere between 300 and 450 feet (91 and 137 m). Roman ruler Julius Caesar described Pharos as a "tower of great height" and of "wonderful construction." The building was destroyed by an earthquake early in the 14th century.

The ancient Romans built lighthouses throughout their vast empire to aid sea trade. Archaeologists have found remains of more than 30. One of the most famous was built at the man-made harbor of Portus, near Ostia, in the first century A.D. Ostia was the seaport that served the city of Rome. The Romans also built two towers in the southern English town of Dover. Only the foundations of the lighthouse built on the western heights of Dover still exist. Remarkably, though, part of the tower erected on the eastern heights still stands.

After the fall of the Roman Empire, about A.D. 476, lighthouse building came to a virtual halt for hundreds of years. During this period (the early Middle Ages), the countries of Europe did not trade much with each other. Without widespread commerce between countries, there was little need for lighthouses. In the eighth and ninth centuries, candles in some buildings, such as monasteries, guided local sailors. In China, pagodas sometimes housed a light to guide sailors. This was the case over 1,000 years ago when a lantern was hung from the Mahota Pagoda to guide vessels sailing along the river near Shanghai.

When trade between European nations picked up again, lighthouse building resumed. The Italians built a lighthouse at the port of Meloria in A.D. 1157. It was one of the first lighthouses in the Western world to be built in the post-Roman period. Hook Head Lighthouse in Ireland was commissioned later in the 12th century. Monks operated the light in the stone tower for over 400 years. After the order was disbanded, the building continued as an aid to navigation. A light continues to shine from Hook Head Lighthouse today.

Despite these successes, lighthouses were still unusual. Just how scarce were they? There may have been as few as 30 lighthouses in the entire world in 1600. Many reasons explained the small number. For a long time, governments simply were not in favor of putting up lighthouses. Military officials feared the lighted towers would help an enemy's army navigate. In some places, "wreckers" did not want a lighthouse built. These people earned a living by salvaging items from shipwrecks. Fewer wrecks would mean a lower income. (To increase the likelihood of a shipwreck, some wreckers even shined lanterns along dangerous parts of the coast to trick sailors into thinking they were near a harbor.) Besides, lighthouses were costly to construct and difficult to maintain. When open fires provided the light source, they consumed an enormous amount of fuel such as wood or coal, night after night. It would take new inventions in lighting technology and an increase in trading between countries before lighthouses would become common.

Colonial Lighthouses

As far as we know, New England was the site of the first lighthouse in the British colonies. When many people think of

Boston in colonial times, they think of Paul Revere and the Sons of Liberty. Long before the Boston Tea Party, however, the city of Boston was a prosperous port. Locating the entrance to the city's harbor was tricky in the 1700s. Colonial ships did not have electric lights or radar technology to help them find their way. Merchants wanted a lighthouse that would help guide ships in and out of the harbor.

On September 14, 1716, a lighthouse was lit on Little Brewster Island, marking the harbor for the first time. It was likely the first lighthouse built in what would become the United States. The stone tower, about 60 feet tall (18 m), was designed to "prevent the loss of the Lives and Estates of His Majesty's Subjects." All ships using the harbor, except the king of England's ships, paid a duty. This tax paid for the construction and upkeep of the lighthouse, just as tolls collected today help governments maintain some bridges and roads. The lighthouse at Boston Harbor was shaped like the main part of a cone. (Picture a birthday party hat with the point cut off.) At the top was a lantern room with glass windows that housed and protected the light source. Candles or crude oil lamps probably provided the light; no records tell us for sure how the tower was first lighted.

The pace of lighthouse building moved slowly in the colonies. Lack of funding was a

A ship flying the British flag sails past the first Boston Harbor Lighthouse built on Little Brewster Island. *U.S. Coast Guard Historian's Office*

big hindrance. With no central government, each colony had to find a way to raise money to build, maintain, and operate lighthouses. Often holding a lottery was the solution. When New York merchants wanted a lighthouse to guide ships into their harbor, it took two lotteries, then a tax on ships entering the port, to make their wish a reality.

New Lighthouses for a New Nation

After breaking free from England, the new country faced many challenges. One of the most urgent was finding a way to support itself. Leaders knew safe harbors would help increase trade, and lighthouses could help. Congress passed a law in 1789 making the federal government responsible for the country's 12 existing lighthouses. The law also gave the national government authority to pay for and build new lighthouses. Its top priority was building a lighthouse at Cape Henry in Virginia.

Ships sailed past the cape, at the mouth of the Chesapeake Bay, to reach the busy ports of Norfolk, Virginia, and Annapolis and Baltimore in Maryland. For decades, people had talked about building a lighthouse there. At times, colonists had lighted wood in a metal basket to mark the point, but pirates easily darkened such beacons. Workers hauled several tons (one ton equals 907 kg) of sandstone to the site before the American Revolution. The war halted the project, and sand gradually covered most of the valuable stone at the windy site. The government hired a builder for a lighthouse at Cape Henry, and ordered a lighthouse built "with all convenient speed." The octagonal stone structure, which still stands, was first lighted in the fall of 1792. (It was not, however, the first lighthouse completed by the federal government. Maine's Portland Head Lighthouse earned that distinction; construction on it started before the federal government was formed. It was first lighted in January 1791.)

At first, lighthouses were erected mainly to guide ships in and out of harbors. Because so much commerce and shipbuilding was being done in New England, more early

The old Cape Henry Lighthouse, rear, is dwarfed by a newer cast iron tower in this photo. *U.S. Coast Guard Historian's Office*

lighthouses were built there than in any other region. It would not take long before officials decided to expand construction beyond harbor entrances. One of the first efforts to do so happened in North Carolina.

Just off the coast of Cape Hatteras, North Carolina, lay several miles of dangerous sandbars called Diamond Shoals. These shoals and the nearby Gulf Stream made sailing in the region hazardous. Ships sailing up the coast sought out the swift currents of the northbound Gulf Stream to speed their

journeys. Southbound ships tried to steer clear of the currents to avoid delays. There was not much room for error when avoiding the fast-moving currents because only a few miles of water lay between the shoals and the Gulf Stream. A 90-foot (27-m)-tall lighthouse at Cape Hatteras was lighted in 1803. For decades, it was considered one of the most important lighthouses in the country.

Powerful Boats and New Waterways

The U.S. lighthouse system grew quickly in the 1800s as the result of two high-tech breakthroughs. Surprisingly, the new technologies had nothing to do with how lighthouses were built. Instead, they affected how and where ships traveled.

In August 1807, onlookers watched in amazement as a strange-looking boat traveled up the Hudson River in New York. Unlike sailing ships, the boat chugged along when there was no wind. Amazingly, it could move just as easily against the tide as with it. Sparks from the wood burning in its boiler lit up the sky and frightened many along the shore.

The newfangled boat traveled 150 miles (241 km) in 32 hours. That seems slow by today's standards when you can travel that far in a car in about two-and-a-half hours. At the time, though, the boat set a new record for speed. Inventor Robert Fulton bragged, "The power of propelling boats by steam is now fully proved." He also predicted the boat would change America by allowing "cheap and quick conveyance" of goods on the Mississippi and other western rivers. Fulton was right.

As settlers moved west, the steamboat made it possible to ship goods cheaply and easily down the Mississippi River to New Orleans. The Louisiana city sits close to where the river flows into the Gulf of Mexico. At the same time, factories in the North and overseas wanted the South's cotton for making textiles. These factors combined to spark a lighthouse-building boom in the Southeast. In the 1830s, several lighthouses were built quickly to light the shores of the Gulf of Mexico in Alabama, Florida, Louisiana, and Mississippi.

The steamboat was also a boon to leisure travel. Steamboat companies sprang up to offer people a chance to cruise a river or bay. Now that boats did not need wind to move, people could rely on a set schedule and plan when they would leave and when they would arrive at a destination. The Chesapeake Bay, the coast of Maine, and the Hudson River were just some of the popular places for steamboat travel along the East Coast. The growing destinations for boats required more lighthouses to keep crews and passengers safe.

The technical know-how to build canals was the other big breakthrough. The most important canal of the era was New York's Erie Canal. Stretching from Buffalo on Lake Erie to Albany on the Hudson River, it was 364 miles long (568 km). The canal made it much easier for settlers to move west. Perhaps more important, it allowed goods from the West to be shipped east for a fraction of the cost of moving them by road. Cities along the canal became boomtowns almost overnight. Buffalo, New York, grew fourfold in the first seven years after the canal opened. The canal also sparked a need for lighthouses along the Hudson. From Albany, ships could sail downriver to New York City.

Lighthouses were needed at Buffalo and other Great Lakes towns to make shipping

The Buffalo Lighthouse was built because of the increase in ship traffic after the Erie Canal was completed. This photo, taken about 1870, shows the tower after it had been raised slightly. *C. L. Pond / Lower Lakes Marine Historical Society*

as safe as possible. "Shipping was vital to all parts of the United States, with lumber going one way and finished products going the other," recalled Anna Bowen, the daughter of a keeper who lived at a Lake Superior lighthouse in the first half of the 20th century. "And it was my family's job to see that the ships passed safely."

As the population of the United States grew, larger boats were built to carry more goods. These bigger boats had deeper drafts, meaning their bottoms reached further into the water than those of earlier vessels. Now sailors had to be warned about rocks and shoals that had not posed a hazard before. There was another reason the nation needed more lighthouses. The steam engines that propelled boats also powered dredging machines. This equipment removed sand and silt from under water to make harbors deeper. Towns without deep natural harbors could now be transformed into successful ports.

Sometimes new industries created demand for lighthouses. In the 1800s, whalebone was used for buggy whips, women's clothes, and umbrellas. Oil obtained from whale blubber fueled street-lights, locomotive headlights, even lamps in lighthouses. In New England, newly built lighthouses helped guide whalers home safely. In several places, lighthouses allowed a region's natural resources to be shipped to other parts of the country. The aptly named Copper Harbor Lighthouse in northern Michigan was one of many that helped the area's copper mining industry thrive.

A Lighthouse Gold Mine

In 1848, a carpenter working in northern California discovered shiny flakes of gold in a streambed. The following year, thousands of gold miners began arriving in San Francisco. Many came by ship, and so did their supplies. At the time, California was lightly populated. It had a long, rugged coastline with only a few natural harbors and no lighthouses.

Before docking in San Francisco, sea captains had to enter San Francisco Bay through the Golden Gate. Fast tides and frequent fog made it tough to navigate this three-mile-wide (5 km) passage. Once inside the bay, the dangerous journey was not over. The rocky ledges of Alcatraz Island posed a serious threat to safe navigation.

In 1851, San Francisco merchants begged officials in Washington, D.C., for a lighthouse. The lack of a lighthouse "has

The first U.S. lighthouse on the West Coast, built on Alcatraz Island, began shining a light in 1854. A taller lighthouse on the famous island in San Francisco Harbor has since replaced it. *Drawing by Major Hartman Bache / U.S. Coast Guard Historian's Office*

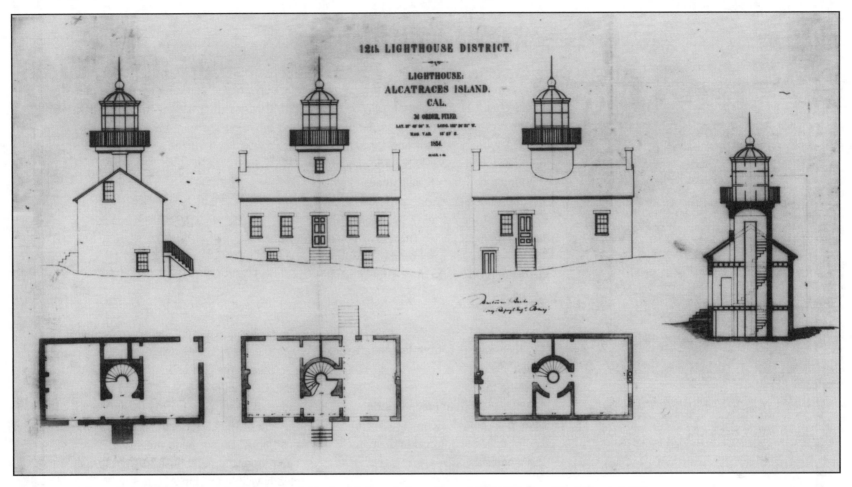

The first 16 lighthouses built on the West Coast had a design much like this lighthouse built on Alcatraz Island. *U.S. Coast Guard Historian's Office*

caused great detention, inconvenience, as well as the total loss of many vessels bound to this port," they wrote. The following year, a lighthouse was built on Alcatraz Island. (The now-famous prison had not been constructed there yet.) The lighthouse was not lighted until 1854 because of budget problems and delays in getting the lighting equipment sent to California. Even so, it was the first U.S. lighthouse in operation on the West Coast. For the next six years, there would be a flurry of construction; 16 lighthouses were built in California, Oregon, and Washington from 1852 to 1858.

New Management

The building boom on the West Coast was not the only event that affected the lighthouse system in 1852. That fall, there was a shake-up in the way the system was run. Official reports had revealed many problems.

25

Why Height Matters

The Point Reyes Lighthouse in California is only 35 feet tall. The light's focal plane is nearly 300 feet, however, because the lighthouse was built on a cliff. *U.S. Coast Guard Historian's Office*

How did builders decide how tall a lighthouse should be? First, they had to determine the distance from which the lighthouse light needed to be visible. Lighthouses marking harbors were not usually very tall because boaters did not need to see them from great distances. By contrast, a major light along the ocean, called a landfall light, would be the first thing sailors spotted after a long voyage. The beams from these lighthouses had to be visible far away to help sailors plot their course toward land.

Once builders knew how far away the lighthouse had to be visible, they could determine how high the lighthouse light needed to be above water. The elevation or height of the center of the beam of light is its focal plane. This easy-to-build model will let you see how the curvature (curving) of the earth affects focal plane.

You'll Need

Pencil
4½-inch-long (11.4-cm-long) craft stick
Tape measure
Masking tape
12-inch (30.5-cm) piece of string
Styrofoam ball, 5 inches (12.7 cm) or
     6 inches (15.2 cm) in diameter
2 pushpins

Draw a line across the short side of the craft stick at its midpoint. Use tape to attach the string to the stick at one end.

Insert the craft stick (a lighthouse) into the middle of the Styrofoam ball (the earth), leaving the end with the string visible. Push the stick down until you can barely see your mark. Put one end of the tape measure against the base of the stick. Stretch the tape measure out along the curve of the ball, and insert one pushpin 2 inches (5 cm) away from the stick and the other pushpin 4½ inches (11.4 cm) away.

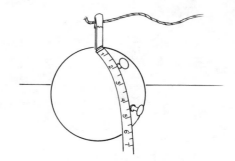

The pushpins represent ships; remove tape measure.

Steady the ball on your thigh or a table by placing one hand on the end of the craft stick. With your free hand, hold the end of the string tight so it rests on pushpin A. Do not bend the string. The beam from the lighthouse (the string) is clearly visible to Ship A, but Ship B would not be able to see it because of the way the earth's surface curves.

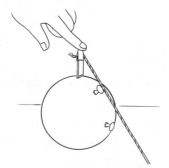

Now let go of the string and pull the craft stick out of the ball as far as it will come (you might need to steady the stick with one hand). Use your other hand to stretch the string tight so it rests on pushpin B.

Would the lighthouse light also be visible to Ship A? What does this tell you about how high the lighthouse light needs to be if you want Ships A and B to see it? After more powerful lights were developed in the 1800s, some lighthouse towers were raised. Why was this necessary? How would the height of a lighthouse built on a hill differ from the height of one built nearby on a flat beach if both lighthouses had to be visible at the same distance?

These engineers were better qualified than most people to pick the best places to build lighthouses. They could help design sturdy structures and make sure lighthouses were well built. They were also eager to adapt the latest building technology to the lighthouse system. Their influence helped the country expand its network of lighthouses to many offshore sites. In the past, it had been impossible to build lighthouses in some of these spots. New building materials also helped change the way lighthouses could be designed and built. As a result, the U.S. lighthouse system grew rapidly in the late 1800s, becoming one of the best in the world.

The End of an Era

By 1920 or so, the pace of lighthouse construction was slowing. By then, lighthouses already stood in many places most hazardous to ships. In other places, a large buoy could be installed to do the job a lighthouse once did. Lighthouses were not as important as they had been in the past because people did not rely as much on boats to carry freight. Railroads had taken over that job.

Even the need for existing lighthouses was declining. New bridges gradually put ferryboats out of business. Some of these bridges included lights bright enough to help boaters, which meant lighthouses could

Some lighthouses were poorly built, and keepers were not always reliable. Lighthouses did not use the most advanced lighting technology available. Stephen Pleasonton, the man who had run the lighthouse system for 32 years, lost his job.

Now a carefully chosen committee would be in charge. The Lighthouse Board, a government organization that included scientists and engineers, overhauled many aspects of the lighthouse system. Run-down

lighthouses were repaired or rebuilt. New technology was installed to create brighter lights, making the coastline safer. The Lighthouse Board also worked hard to hire qualified keepers and checked to see if they did a good job. For better control, the nation's lighthouses were organized into 12 regions, known as districts. A military officer, often an engineer, was in charge of each district.

WHO COULD BE A U.S. LIGHTHOUSE KEEPER?

Getting a job as keeper once had little to do with a person's ability to do the job. For over a century, some people became keepers simply because they owned land where a lighthouse was built. Others were war veterans who were rewarded for their efforts with a steady job after the war. Many keepers, though, were appointed when politicians recommended them for the job. Some keepers who were selected this way performed well. Others did not. Under this system, keepers came and went frequently. In fact, a keeper could be ousted every time a president of a different political party took office. A writer made fun of this system by describing a lighthouse as a building where the government "maintains a lamp and the friend of a politician." The practice lasted until the late 1800s.

Overall, the government made the keepers' job requirements more formal after the middle of the 19th century. Detailed records were required, so keepers had to be able to read and write well. The government checked qualifications of would-be keepers and kept a closer watch on those who did not do a good job. Since elections did not force an automatic change, some keepers held jobs at the same station for decades.

The Coast Guard, a branch of the military, took over the lighthouse system in 1939. At the time, keepers were given the option of joining the Coast Guard or remaining as civilian keepers.

Today, machines operate all U.S. lighthouses. Boston Light now has a civilian keeper who works with Coast Guard volunteers and the National Park Service to keep the station in good order and greet visitors.

be closed. Boaters also began to depend on electronic systems instead of lights from lighthouses. Even so, the government continued to rely on floating lighthouses, or lightships, in places where building a lighthouse would have been difficult. In 1960, the government began to build structures called "Texas towers," which replaced lightships. Today, huge buoys and smaller towers have taken the place of most Texas towers.

The last traditional U.S. lighthouse with an enclosed lantern room was built in 1962. Charleston Lighthouse was constructed on an island near Charleston, South Carolina. From a distance, it looks a bit like a sturdy prison guard tower. Unlike many lighthouse towers, it is triangular. Made of aluminum and steel, it can withstand winds up to 160 miles (257 km) per hour. Charleston Lighthouse is distinctive for another reason. It is the only lighthouse in the United States with an elevator.

Today when lights are needed in new places, a high-tech aid to navigation is built. This often consists of a small, powerful light on top of a structure that resembles a cell phone tower. Some old lighthouses also continue to guide boaters. Today, there is one big difference at lighthouses from the era when children grew up helping their parents tend the lights: machines, not people, keep the lights burning.

Decorate a Lighthouse Cake

The lighthouse at Cape Lookout, North Carolina, shown here in 1951, is distinguished by large black diamonds painted on the tower. *U.S. Coast Guard Historian's Office*

As the lighthouse system expanded, the government needed a way for sailors to tell nearby lighthouses apart during the day. The solution was to use certain paint colors or paint patterns to create a distinctive look, known as a daymark. You can decorate a lighthouse cake and create your own unique daymark.

Adult supervision required

You'll Need

Box of yellow or white cake mix
9 × 13-inch (22.9 × 33-cm) cake pan
Can of vanilla frosting
Knife for frosting cake
Ruler or tape measure
¼ cup (.24 metric cup) graham cracker crumbs (Plain crumbs work best for sand; plain and chocolate ones mixed will give a rockier appearance to your shoreline.)
Bag of black licorice twists or chocolate twists
12-oz bag mini M&Ms
Assorted decorative sprinkles
4–6 small lemon gumdrops

Prepare and bake the cake as directed. After it cools, remove it from pan and frost it. Turn the cake so the 9-inch (22.9-cm) side is parallel to the edge of your work surface. Use the ruler to measure the bottom two inches (5.1 cm) of the cake. Mark off this area by running your knife through the frosting. Pour the graham cracker crumbs in the area you have marked off. Don't worry about getting some above the line; unevenness will give your beach or cliff a more natural look.

Take two chocolate or licorice twists and place them in the middle of the cake in vertical lines to form the walls of a lighthouse. One end of each twist should just touch the graham cracker crumbs. For a rectangular tower, align the twists as straight as possible. To give your tower a cone-shaped appearance, angle the twists slightly so the opening at the top is not as wide as the opening at the bottom.

Next, cut a piece of chocolate or licorice twist to put across the top of your tower. It should extend about ½-inch (1.3-cm) beyond each side of your lighthouse to create the appearance of a walkway around the lantern room. Cut three 2-inch (5.1-cm) pieces of twist to make the sides and top of a lantern room. Form a tight circle with the gumdrops in the center of the lantern room for the light.

Use smaller pieces of licorice to add a decorative pattern; fill in with the mini M&Ms and sprinkles to make a unique daymark for your lighthouse. Or, re-create the daymark of a famous lighthouse. For Whitefish Shoal in Michigan, form red spiral stripes. West Quoddy Head in Maine has red horizontal bands. North Carolina's Cape Hatteras sports black spiral stripes, while nearby Cape Lookout is decorated with black diamonds.

Chapter Three

A Field Guide to U.S. Lighthouses

Your idea of what a lighthouse looks like may depend on where you live or where you have traveled. If you have walked along some of the sandy beaches of the eastern United States, you may think of lighthouses as tall, round towers. On the West Coast, though, many lighthouses are short structures built on steep cliffs. Along the Great Lakes, it is common to see a lighthouse (or two) at the end of a long pier. In a few cases, short lighthouses have been constructed atop military forts.

Not all lighthouses are located in remote areas. The skyline of New York City is visible from the Robbins Reef Lighthouse in New York Harbor. *U.S. Coast Guard Historian's Office*

As you might have guessed, there is no such thing as a typical lighthouse. Lighthouses built in the middle of water usually look different from ones on land. Those designed to help sailors find their bearings far off the coast tend to be taller than those built on lakes and rivers.

Just as certain styles of clothes are "in" at one time and not another, so too are ways of designing buildings. Building materials, like fabrics, also change over time. For these reasons, a lighthouse built at the end of the 18th century is likely to look different from one built at the end of the 19th century. The amount of money available for construction also affected the appearance of a lighthouse.

Lighthouses can be split into two basic groups: land-based lighthouses and offshore lighthouses. This field guide will help you identify the different types of lighthouses in the United States.

Land-Based Lighthouses

Land-based lighthouses can be placed in categories depending on what they are made of.

Brick and Stone Masonry Lighthouses

There were 12 lighthouses in our country in 1789, and all were made from wood or stone. The first towers were made from stones of various sizes collected near the

Build a Lighthouse Model That Lights Up

Create a lighthouse model for school or home that your friends and teachers will love. Your model will have a light shining from the lantern room just like a real lighthouse.

You'll Need

Old newspapers
Plastic knife
Ruler
2 16-inch (40.6-cm) pieces of #18 insulated wire
9 x 3 ⅞-inch (22.9 x 9.8-cm) Styrofoam cone (from a craft store)
Acrylic craft paints and paintbrushes (optional)
Tacky craft glue
Thick piece of cardboard, about 12 x 12 inches (30.5 x 30.5 cm)
Plastic lid about 3½ inches (8.9 cm) in diameter (from a small margarine container)
Small socket with lightbulb (from hobby or hardware store)
Pencil
Scissors
White roll of electrical tape, ¾-inch (1.9-cm) width
6 brass paper fasteners
D battery, unless directions for socket call for another type

4-ounce (13-gram) lidless clear plastic container (single-serving applesauce cup works well)

Place several newspapers on your work surface for protection. Use the knife to remove about 1 inch (2.5 cm) of protective coating from both ends of both pieces of wire. Be careful to cut into the coating but not the wire; scrape coating off by pushing the knife slowly away from you or pulling the wire toward you while holding the knife steady.

Use the knife to cut the top 2 inches or so (5.1 cm) off the Styrofoam cone.

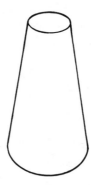

If you choose to paint your lighthouse, do so now. Put on thick layers of paint because Styrofoam is absorbent; let dry.

Glue the bottom of the cone anywhere on the cardboard.

Place plastic lid on work surface with writing face down. Position socket in the lid's center; trace around the socket with your pencil. Set socket aside.

Hold the lid with one hand, and use scissors to poke two small slits in the plastic lid on opposite sides of the circle. (Be careful; this is best done with scissor blades open.) Next, feed one piece of wire from below until an inch or so of wire sticks through the top of the lid. You may need to hold the slit open with your fingers while you feed the wire through. Feed the other wire through the second slit. Glue socket to the lid within the circle you traced without letting wire slip through the slits.

When dry, attach one end of one wire tightly to one connection of the socket; use tape if necessary to form a tight connection. Do the same with the other wire. Glue the lid/socket to the top of the cone; let dry.

Pull tightly on one wire until it rests snugly against the cone. Secure the wire to the cone with three paper fasteners by sticking a prong into the cone on either side of the wire.

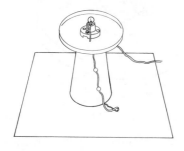

Use the same method to attach the other wire to the cone.

With tape, attach the end of one wire to either end of the battery. Tape the battery (lying on its side) to the cardboard. Test your circuit by touching the end of the free piece of wire to the battery. If the bulb does not light up, recheck your connections to make sure they are secure.

Turn the plastic container upside down over the socket to form the lantern room. Use a few pieces of rolled up tape to create a hinge to attach the container to the lid.

Do not tape on all sides in case you need to adjust the connections or replace the bulb.

What types of empty containers could you use to add a keeper's house, oil house, and boathouse to your model?

building site. Later, stones were cut to a precise size and shape to make sturdier buildings. Before the 1850s, most brick and stone lighthouses were less than 90 feet (27 m) tall because builders did not think they could make taller buildings sturdy. Construction crews instead used wide bases to stabilize the structures. The taller the lighthouse, the wider its base had to be to support the weight of its walls. (Early skyscrapers also were built this way.)

After the Lighthouse Board took over in 1852, it authorized construction of tall brick lighthouses, or those higher than 150 feet (46 m). Fifteen tall brick towers were built along the Atlantic Coast. All were cone-shaped, except for the six-sided tower at Cape Romain, North Carolina. Among those still standing are some of the most famous lighthouses in the United States.

Examples: Cape Hatteras Lighthouse, North Carolina (tall brick); Georgetown Lighthouse, South Carolina (brick); Sandy Hook Lighthouse, New Jersey (stone)

Wooden Lighthouses

Wood was plentiful in the colonies and was used to build some of the first lighthouses. As you might expect, wooden towers were not very durable. Strong storms could destroy them, and they burned easily. Brick and stone lighthouses often replaced damaged wooden ones. Despite its drawbacks, wood was used to build some lighthouses into the 20th century.

Examples: Hereford Inlet Lighthouse, New Jersey; Mukilteo Lighthouse, Washington; Old Mission Point Lighthouse, Michigan

A Washington State ferry navigates near the wooden Mukilteo Lighthouse. The lighthouse was built in 1906. *Darlene Cook / Mukilteo Historical Society*

Cast-Iron Lighthouses

Have you ever tried to lift a cast-iron frying pan? Chances are you could not move it with only one hand. Today, newer materials have made it possible to make lighter skillets. Back in the 19th century, plenty of pans were made of cast iron, and so were large stoves heated by fires. Cast iron's usefulness extended far beyond the home. It turned out to be a sturdy building material for lighthouses.

Built in 1764 of stone, the lighthouse at Sandy Hook, New Jersey, is the oldest existing lighthouse in the United States. *U.S. Coast Guard Historian's Office*

TWO OF A KIND: THE STORY OF TWIN LIGHTS

Until the late 1700s, there was no good way to tell one light-house light from another. That's because lighthouses had only fixed lights, meaning that a steady light shined from each lantern room. In 1781, the first rotating light in the world was installed in Sweden, producing a flashing light. Before flashing lights were common, officials sometimes put up two lighthouses in one spot to help sailors figure out their location. In such cases, the lighthouses were known as twin lights.

The first twin lights in the United States were built in colonial America at Plymouth, Massachusetts. Erected in 1769 at Gurnet Point, the twin lights were small lantern rooms placed at either end of a rectangular house. Other well-known twin lights include those at Cape Elizabeth, Maine; Cape Ann, Massachusetts; and Navesink, New Jersey. In one case, the government built three lighthouses near each other on Cape Cod in Massachusetts. They became known as the Three Sisters of Nauset. In 1924, the government converted all of its stations with more than one lighthouse to a single light. In some cases, one of the towers was torn down or was moved.

These towers at Plymouth, Massachusetts, were completed in 1843. Only one tower remains at the site today. *U.S. Coast Guard Historian's Office*

Why? Even though cast iron forms heavy pans, it is lighter than stone or brick, making it handy for lighthouses built on piers and breakwaters. (Engineers did not want to damage a pier by putting a heavy lighthouse on it.) Cast-iron could be shipped to a building site in the shape of a cylinder or as thin plates that could be bolted together quickly. Cast-iron lighthouses were simple to take apart and put back together, so they could be moved easily if necessary. Plus, cast iron does not corrode as easily as other metals, which cut down on maintenance work.

Many cast-iron lighthouses were built in the shape of short, conical towers. Some were lined with brick for stability. A cast-iron pier lighthouse might be combined with a keeper's house to form a compact structure. Cast iron was also popular for making key parts of lighthouses, even if the structure itself was not made from cast iron. When you see metal doors, windows, railings, and lantern rooms on an old lighthouse, there is a good chance they are made of cast iron. The first cast-iron lighthouse in the United States was built on Long Island Head in Boston Harbor in 1844.

Examples: New Cape Henry Lighthouse, Virginia (cast iron lined with brick); Nobska Lighthouse, Massachusetts, (cast iron lined with brick); Portland Breakwater Lighthouse, Maine (pier light)

RANGE LiGHTS

The Grand Haven pier lights in Grand Haven, Michigan, function as range lights. The raised walkway, or catwalk, was built so keepers could reach the lighthouse at the end of the pier when waves were high. *Dave Kenyon / Michigan Department of Natural Resources*

Two lighthouses built near each other are not always twin lights. Instead, range lights help guide ships in and out of harbors or along narrow channels. The front range light is placed closest to the water and is lower in elevation than its partner, the rear range light. When ships can see the lights from both lighthouses, one atop the other, sailors know that they are in the right place to sail safely into the harbor or though the channel. If the rear light appears to the right or left of the front light, the sailor must change his position. Range lights are also known as leading lights or guiding lights. They are especially common along the Great Lakes and in the Atlantic provinces of Canada. One of the most unusual pairs of range lights in the United States exists today in Beverly, Massachusetts. The front range light shines from the Hospital Point Lighthouse, a brick structure built in the 1870s. The rear range light shines from the steeple of a church about one mile (1.6 km) away.

Iron and Steel Skeletal Towers

One of the easiest types of lighthouses to identify is the skeletal lighthouse. Just as X-rays show us our bones under our skin, skeletal lighthouses are towers without protective walls. These towers resemble today's high-tension power line towers and some cell phone towers. The only enclosed parts of a skeletal lighthouse are the lantern room and a central column holding a staircase. The watch room below the lantern room is often, but not always, enclosed. The rest of the building is constructed of metal rods. Used at first for lighthouses built in open water, this design was then adapted for use on land. Skeletal lighthouses come in different configurations and heights. They were sometimes used for the taller rear light in a pair of range lights.

Examples: Coney Island Lighthouse, New York; Sanibel Island Lighthouse, Florida; Whitefish Point Lighthouse, Michigan

Concrete Lighthouses

It is hard to pass a construction site today without spotting a concrete mixer. Concrete is sturdy, holds up to harsh weather, and is relatively inexpensive. Concrete began to replace brick towers at the beginning of the 20th century. Many lighthouses along the West Coast and in Alaska and Hawaii are made of concrete. Reinforced concrete (con-

The skeletal lighthouse at Whitefish Point, Michigan, as it appeared in 1913. *U.S. Coast Guard Historian's Office*

38

crete made stronger by metal bars) was used in the 20th century for lighthouses in areas prone to earthquakes. The first reinforced concrete lighthouse in the country was built at Point Arena, California, in 1908. Concrete lighthouses tend to have white, smooth walls, but they can be confused with brick lighthouses covered by stucco.

Examples: Cape Spencer Lighthouse, Alaska; Cleveland East Ledge Lighthouse, Massachusetts; Kilauea Point Lighthouse, Hawaii

Offshore Lighthouses

By the early 1850s, there were 331 lighthouses in the United States. Although the system was growing quickly, there were still plenty of places where lighthouses had not been built. Many of these sites were in the middle of the water or on wave-swept rocks. Conditions made construction hazardous, expensive, and, sometimes, impossible. At first, the government used "light boats" to mark offshore spots. Sometimes referred to as floating lights, these sturdy ships were anchored in one place. Bright lights shining from their masts warned sailors of nearby hazards.

Lightships, however, were not the perfect solution. They were expensive to operate because they required a complete crew instead of only one or two keepers. Storms

or collisions with other boats could damage or sink lightships. When a lightship was being repaired, there was not always another one that could be moved into its place.

In the middle of the 1800s, new engineering know-how made it possible to replace some lightships with offshore lighthouses. (It would take over a century, though, before all the lightships in the United States were taken out of service.) Offshore lighthouses are distinguished by the type of foundation they have. Even lighthouses on the same foundation can vary widely in appearance.

Straight Pile vs. Screw Pile Foundation

In some locations on land and offshore, construction workers drilled piles, or support poles, into rock or soil to support a lighthouse. Straight pile foundations were made of wood at first, then iron. Builders learned that straight pile foundations were not nearly as stable in soft and sandy soils, though. Amazingly, a blind engineer found a better way to build foundations in soft soil. In the 1830s, Irish-born Alexander Mitchell worked with his son, also an engineer, to develop the screw pile foundation. He first used the technique in Scotland as a way to moor ships. Mitchell described his invention as "a bar of iron having at its lower extremity a broad plate or disk of metal in a spiral . . . on the principle of a screw." Imagine an oversized

corkscrew; now you have a good idea what the tip of a screw pile foundation looked like.

Mitchell tested out his idea on a lighthouse in the River Thames, and it worked. His experimental lighthouse had nine iron piles with 4-foot-wide (1.2 m) screws at their ends. The oversized screws were driven 22 feet (7 m) below the riverbed. The open foundation provided little resistance to wind and waves, so bad storms and high seas were less likely to damage it.

After the Civil War, the screw pile foundation became popular in the United States. (It is not possible to tell a screw pile foundation apart from a straight pile foundation just by looking at it.) The screw pile foundation was used mainly for lighthouses built on rivers and protected bays. A hexagonal or octagonal wooden cottage often was placed on top of the screw pile foundation. The one-and-a-half-story house had dormer windows; a short lantern room protruded from the center of its metal roof. The cottage-style screw pile lighthouse was most popular in the Chesapeake Bay, the sounds of North Carolina, and along the Gulf Coast.

Examples: Seven Foot Knoll Lighthouse, Maryland (screw pile); Southwest Reef Lighthouse, Louisiana; (straight pile); Thomas Point Shoal Lighthouse, Maryland (screw pile, and the last one on the Chesapeake Bay in its original location)

Inset: The screw pile lighthouse takes its name from the large screws used to help it stand in soft, sandy soils.
U.S. Coast Guard Historian's Office

Above: Maryland's Hooper Straight Lighthouse, seen here in 1915, is a typical cottage-style screw pile lighthouse. It has since been moved ashore and is part of a museum. *U.S. Coast Guard Historian's Office*

away than those in bays, so the towers would need to be taller. More powerful lighting equipment was large and heavy, requiring strong towers with solid foundations to support them.

The government selected Carysfort Reef, off the coast of Miami, Florida, as the location of a new type of lighthouse. George Meade, an engineer who later fought in the Civil War, helped to build the 450-ton lighthouse (408 metric tons). He tinkered with the design of a typical screw pile foundation by adding round cast-iron disks, each six feet (1.8 m) wide, above the screw tip. The disks spread the weight of the tower over a larger area. Exposed screw pile lighthouses featured a skeletal tower. Since these lighthouses were located in the middle of water, builders enclosed a keeper's quarters within the skeletal framework.

Examples: Fowey Rocks, Florida; Ship Shoal, Louisiana

Caisson Foundation

On a cold January night in 1893, a couple of boys carefully climbed an icy cherry tree in their yard in Virginia. From their position, they could look out over the frozen Chesapeake Bay. What they saw, and more important, what they didn't see, frightened them. The brothers had hoped to see a light shining from Wolf Trap Light, a cottage

Exposed Screw Pile Foundation

Coral reefs lurking below the turquoise water of the Florida Keys could damage vessels, or, worse, make them sink. Hurricanes blowing through the area brought strong waves and high winds. Sadly, an 1846 hurricane destroyed a traditional stone light-

house on Sand Key. The lighthouse keeper and her five children drowned.

Engineers thought screw pile foundations might work in the Florida Keys. First, they realized that the short screw pile lighthouses used in protected bays and rivers would need to be changed. Lighthouses in the Keys needed to be seen from farther

The Carysfort Reef Lighthouse, as it looked in 1962, stands watch over a treacherous area in the Florida Keys. *U.S. Coast Guard Historian's Office*

screw pile lighthouse. "All across the Bay was only blackness," their sister recalled many years later. "We knew the lighthouse must have been carried away. We were afraid Papa must have been lost, too."

At the time, they had no way of knowing that their father, the keeper, had escaped. The lighthouse was not as fortunate. Ripped from its moorings by ice, it was discovered floating down the bay. Ice clearly could be fatal to a screw pile lighthouse. For this reason, the Lighthouse Board began to replace these lighthouses with costlier caisson lighthouses in the late 1800s.

Like the screw pile, the caisson lighthouse takes its name from its foundation, not the style of lighthouse built atop it. The term *caisson* usually refers to a large cast-iron tube with a wooden grill or watertight layer at its bottom. Caissons could also be made from wood. Open at the top, the caisson was sunk into a sandy or muddy sea bottom by filling it with concrete and/or rocks. Workers assembled the bottom of the caisson foundations and part of the tube on land. As the caisson sunk in the water, more layers of cast iron plates were added to complete the tube.

Many lighthouses built on caissons were round cast-iron structures much like their foundations. These structures earned the nickname "spark plug" or "coffeepot" because of their appearance. Caisson foundations were most popular in places where

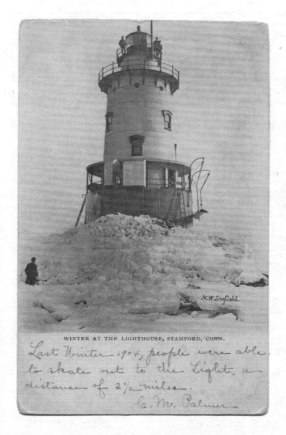

WINTER AT THE LIGHTHOUSE, STAMFORD, CONN.

Last Winter 1904, people were able to skate out to the Light, a distance of 2½ miles.
C. M. Palmer

Connecticut's Stamford Harbor Lighthouse, a typical caisson lighthouse, as depicted on an old postcard. The writer notes that the harbor froze over in the winter of 1904, and people could walk the two-and-one-half miles to the lighthouse. *Author's Collection*

Massachusetts was the first caisson lighthouse in the United States.

Examples: Brandywine Shoal Lighthouse, New Jersey; Sandy Point Shoal Lighthouse, Maryland; Stamford Harbor Lighthouse, Stamford, Connecticut

Pneumatic Caisson Foundation

In rare cases where sea bottoms were very soft or uneven, the dangerous and costly pneumatic caisson was required to secure the foundation. (You cannot tell a pneumatic caisson foundation apart from an ordinary caisson by looking at it.) Pneumatic refers to the use of compressed air to create an underwater working chamber. We use compressed air to inflate tires and power many tools today. Unlike traditional caissons, pneumatic caissons had a top, but no bottom.

Examples: Fourteen Foot Bank Lighthouse, Delaware; Plum Beach Lighthouse, Rhode Island; Sabine Bank Lighthouse, Texas

Wave-Swept Towers

These structures were built on underwater ledges or rocks that were covered by water most of the time. Often, massive stones were fitted together like a jigsaw puzzle to form a solid foundation. Wave-swept lighthouses were expensive and dangerous to build.

THE MULTIPURPOSE LIGHTHOUSE

When is a lighthouse more than a lighthouse? When it also includes a place for the keeper to live. In such cases, the house is said to be integrated, or combined, with the lighthouse. Some of these structures resembled ordinary houses with a tower jutting out of the roofs. That was true of the first 16 U.S. lighthouses built on the West Coast. In other cases, the combined building looked more like a traditional round tower. Such was the case at many offshore caisson lighthouses. Think about the difficulties of arranging furniture in your bedroom if the outer walls of your house were curved!

moving chunks of ice could damage less sturdy structures. They were used mainly on the East Coast from the Chesapeake Bay, north to the coast of Maine. The top of a caisson foundation is visible above water, so these lighthouses are easy to spot. Built in 1871, the Duxbury Pier Lighthouse in

Beginning in 1960, the Coast Guard built a handful of Texas tower lighthouses. These structures were modeled after offshore oil rigs. A light on top of a skeletal tower stands in one corner of these flat steel platforms. The rest of the area is left open to serve as a helicopter landing pad. Helicopters allow Coast Guard personnel to come and go more quickly and safely than by boat.

Workers assemble the caisson for the Sabine Bank, Texas, Lighthouse. The structure no longer stands. *U.S. Coast Guard Historian's Office*

In 1965, the new Texas tower lighthouse replaced the *Chesapeake* lightship on the Chesapeake Bay. *U.S. Coast Guard Historian's Office*

Examples: Mile Rock Lighthouse, California; Minot's Ledge Lighthouse, Massachusetts; St. George Reef Lighthouse, California

Crib Foundation

The crib foundation consisted of a wooden crib, or box, which was sunk into the water with rocks. The top was capped with concrete, and a lighthouse was built on top of the concrete. The crib foundation was a good solution for offshore sites with a hard rock bottom. It was used mainly along the Great Lakes.

Examples: Spectacle Reef Lighthouse, Michigan; Stannard Rock Lighthouse, Michigan

Create a Sponge Painting

The household sponge you use to wipe up spills is made in a factory, but it is actually modeled after the sea creature of the same name. Much of the nation's sponge harvesting occurs near the town of Tarpon Springs, Florida. The nearby Anclote Key Lighthouse, built in 1887, helped the town and its sponge industry flourish. Synthetic sponges have many uses, but some people prefer natural sponges for decorating and applying makeup, among other uses. You can create a lighthouse painting using a natural sponge. Sponges are ideal for seascapes because they can provide nice texture to your work.

Draw your seascape on drawing paper, making more than one sketch if necessary. By their nature, sponge paintings are not precise, so make only a basic outline to guide you when painting. (You can add details later with the paintbrush.)

Cover a work area with newspapers, and pour small quantities of paint onto the plates. Immerse your sponge in water, then squeeze it out. Dip the sponge lightly in the paint color needed for the top of your seascape. Tip: a little paint goes a long way, and a saturated sponge will not transfer as much texture to the paper. Blend colors first by stirring with the paintbrush before dipping sponge in paint.

Work from top to bottom to fill in your painting. After painting is nearly dry, add details with your paintbrush.

You'll Need

Pencil with eraser

Drawing paper, 9 × 12 inch (22.9 × 30.5 cm), or other paper that can be painted

Old newspapers

Plastic or paper cup filled with water

Natural sponges (from craft stores and art supply stores)

Assorted acrylic or tempera paints and disposable plates

Small paintbrush

Chapter Four

Amazing Construction Stories

Lighthouse keepers were not the only people whose hard work helped to keep sailors safe. Long before keepers and their families could tend the light, construction workers performed heroic feats, too. Men who built lighthouses (and it was only men back then) shared common challenges. They battled the weather and sometimes the seas as they labored in remote areas. Some workers on wave-swept rocks died; others in the South got sick from malaria. Most of the lighthouses in this country were built using hand tools considered crude by today's standards. Despite these drawbacks, workers prevailed. Here are the amazing stories behind the construction of four important lighthouses in the United States.

Fourteen Foot Bank Lighthouse, Delaware

Jellyfish, horseshoe crabs, and flounder all call the Delaware Bay home. In the summer of 1885, another creature known as the "sand hog" inhabited part of the bay. A sand hog may sound like a pig enjoying a day at the beach, but it's not. Instead, it was a slang term given to some of the men who helped build the Fourteen Foot Bank Lighthouse.

Since 1876, a lightship had warned sailors away from the Fourteen Foot Bank Shoal. But a light vessel was not practical, since winter ice drove the boat from its post periodically. Now the government wanted a caisson lighthouse to mark the hazardous spot. Up until this point, caisson lighthouses built in the United States consisted of a tube sunk by the weight of rocks and concrete. At Fourteen Foot Bank, workers would use a different method.

For starters, they bolted an iron cylinder to the top of a wooden box that had no bottom and sunk it to the bottom of the bay. Next, workers pumped out the water by fill-

ing the box with just the right amount of compressed air. The result was a working chamber on the bottom of the seabed. You can create a similar effect by turning an empty drinking glass upside down and pushing it to the bottom of a bowl of water. The use of compressed air to create a working chamber had been used successfully to build foundations for bridges, including the famed Brooklyn Bridge. Fourteen Foot Bank Lighthouse would be the first U.S. lighthouse with a caisson foundation sunk by the pneumatic method.

Sand hogs worked in the chamber, digging out sand so the caisson could be submerged further. Their job was dangerous. They entered and exited the chamber through a small passage called the air lock. There, air pressure was increased when the men got ready to go to work. If enough air did not get pumped into the chamber, water could rush in and drown them! Even though the change was made gradually, workers suffered painful headaches and nosebleeds. When sand hogs left the working chamber, the pressure in the air lock was lowered to equal the air pressure above water.

The men also faced a serious hazard called "caisson disease." Today we know the painful condition as "the bends." It can afflict scuba divers who surface too fast, and it can be deadly. The deeper the caisson

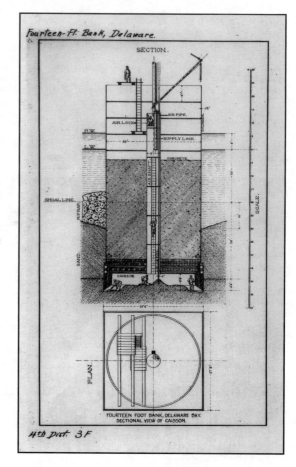

This cross-section of the Fourteen Foot Bank Lighthouse shows the air lock and the chamber where the sand hogs worked. *U.S. Coast Guard Historian's Office*

went, the more time the sand hogs needed to spend in the air lock on the way back to the surface to avoid the condition. Because people did not know as much about the bends in the 19th century as we do today, caisson workers were prone to falling ill from it.

The Fourteen Foot Bank Lighthouse sometime before 1939. It has since been painted white. *U.S. Coast Guard Historian's Office*

Three groups of eight strong men each toiled in the caisson for four hours straight. After a break for meals, they worked another four hours. Caisson workers of that era often wore only pants and boots to cope with warm temperatures and used picks and shovels to chip away at the seabed. The compressed air made it hard to talk; when they did, their voices sounded faint. The men used only candles to guide their work in the dim chamber. Dense fog also made their jobs tough. The fog formed when air pressure blew out the sand they had shoveled. The fog was so thick that the workers

Does Water Pressure Change with Depth?

Have you ever jumped into the pool and had your ears feel like they were being squeezed? Have you tried to stop running water from coming out of a faucet and been surprised how hard you had to push? In both instances, you have felt the effects of water pressure. Divers who placed rocks in position for underwater foundations of lighthouses had to cope with water pressure. So did the workers who sunk caissons with the pneumatic method. In this simple experiment, you can see whether pressure changes as water gets deeper.

You'll Need

Empty plastic milk carton or soda
    bottle (1- or 2-liter)
Ruler
Pushpin
Masking Tape

Use the pushpin to make three holes in the bottle in a straight vertical line. Make the first hole about 3 inches (7.6 cm) from the top of the bottle. Form another hole about 2 inches (5.1 cm) from the bottom, and pierce a third hole between the other two. Be sure to twist the pushpin around a few times to create holes big enough for water to flow through.

Cover holes with tape. Stand over a sink or bathtub as you fill the bottle with water. Remove the tape, and watch the water squirt out. The water coming from the bottom hole should shoot the farthest. What does this tell you about the relationship between water pressure and depth? What challenges would this create for workers building offshore lighthouses?

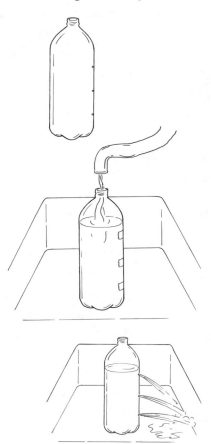

could only see objects about two feet (.6 m) away.

Sinking the caisson was agonizingly slow. It moved downward at a rate of only one or two feet (.3 m to .6 m) a day. As it went down, workers above water increased the height of the iron cylinder, which was filled with concrete. In the fall of 1885, the sand hogs' backbreaking work was done. The caisson now rested more than 33 feet (10 m) below the surface of the shoal. Before leaving for the winter, workers put up a temporary beacon and keeper's house. A permanent cast-iron keeper's house with a tower was installed the following year. The Fourteen Foot Bank Lighthouse still helps sailors navigate the Delaware Bay.

Minot's Ledge Lighthouse, Massachusetts

Isaac Dunham was uneasy. It was April 6, 1850, and a storm was raging around the Minot's Ledge Lighthouse, southeast of Boston. Although he had lived at the offshore tower for only a few months, he knew what a dangerous place it could be. A gale in January had knocked keepers out of bed and sloshed water out of buckets. On this spring evening, strong winds and high seas caused the lighthouse to "reel like a drunken man." Dunham feared the newly built lighthouse might fall into the cold,

The first Minot's Ledge Lighthouse near Cohasset, Massachusetts. *U.S. Coast Guard Historian's Office*

dark waters of the Atlantic Ocean.

Dunham was lucky; the 75-foot (23-m)-tall lighthouse remained standing. But after the government refused to modify the structure in any way, Dunham quit. In April 1851, another storm hit the area. Dunham's replacement had gone to Boston on business, leaving two assistants behind. On April 16, the men wrote, "The lighthouse won't stand over tonight, she shakes 2 feet

each way now." They stuffed their note in a bottle and tossed it into the angry sea. Sometime that night, the tower's iron piles snapped, and the lighthouse crashed into the sea. Both men died.

Congress demanded to learn more about the tragedy. One month later, it appointed a commission to investigate the nation's lighthouses. The group's 1852 report confirmed that there were many problems with the lighthouse system. When a committee known as the Lighthouse Board took charge, one of their first projects was to find a permanent way to mark Minot's Ledge. (Lightships had been used after the collapse of the first tower.)

Funding for a new lighthouse was approved in 1852, and construction began in 1855. This time, local residents would get their wish for a solid tower similar to the Eddystone Lighthouse in England. Work was dangerous and slow. In 1856, iron scaffolding was constructed on the rock. General B. S. Alexander of the U.S. Army Corps of Engineers supervised construction. He wrote, "every workman had something within his reach to lay hold of when a wave would break over the rock, thus doing away with the constant apprehension of danger."

Alexander also set strict rules to make sure his workers were safe. No one was hired unless he could swim and manage a small boat. A lifeboat was always stationed nearby

Workers build the second Minot's Ledge Lighthouse. *U.S. Coast Guard Historian's Office*

(12 m) of the tower were solid except for a round well in the middle for storing water.

Poet Henry Wadsworth Longfellow visited the lighthouse in 1871. He wrote, "We find ourselves at the base of the lighthouse, rising sheer out of the sea like a huge stone cannon, mouth upward." Water has splashed over the top of the lantern room many times during storms. Even so, the tower

Waves swirl around the second Minot's Ledge Lighthouse during a storm. *U.S. Coast Guard Historian's Office*

while men worked on the rock. When a big wave approached, a lookout would holler "Roller coming!" A setback occurred in January 1857 when a ship was thrown against the ledge in a storm. The scaffolding was broken, and the rock itself was shattered. As a result, it took extra time to get the foundation just right. The opportunities for construction work were limited. Men could not work during the winter, while storms raged, or when seas were high. It would take three years to excavate the ledge for the tower's foundation.

Meanwhile, the government purchased a nearby island for a staging area. There, granite from Quincy, Massachusetts, was cut and assembled to make sure the pieces interlocked properly. After workers marked each one carefully, the stones were sent by boat to Minot's Ledge. On the rock, the foundation stones were attached to the ledge with iron bolts that extended 12 inches (30.5 cm) into the rock. The bottom 40 feet

DEFEATS AND TRIUMPHS AT EDDYSTONE

The men who built the second Minot's Ledge Lighthouse owed much of their success to an Englishman they never met. In 1756, John Smeaton was chosen to build a lighthouse on Eddystone Reef, near Plymouth, England. The wave-washed rock had not been kind to three previous attempts at the site.

In the late 1600s, a frustrated ship owner named Henry Winstanley built the first lighthouse on the reef after losing at least one ship there. Waves toppled the lighthouse during its first winter, so he raised the tower, doubled its base, and made other improvements. Winstanley was confident about the durability of the new structure—so confident that he boasted of wanting to be at the lighthouse during the greatest storm ever. In November 1703, he got his wish when a powerful hurricane hit. Afterward, a few twisted iron rods were the only remaining evidence of a lighthouse. Winstanley, his crew, and the keepers were never heard from again.

Less than three years later, John Rudyerd designed a stone and wood tower for the site. For extra strength, he encased it in wooden planks, having been inspired by shipbuilding methods of the day. His design proved successful, but the tower burned in December 1755.

John Smeaton's Eddystone Lighthouse was one of several lighthouses to mark the Eddystone Reef, near Plymouth, England. *U.S. Coast Guard Historian's Office*

Enter John Smeaton. When he tackled the job, many people thought another wood tower would suit the site. They believed a wood structure would have the "give" to sway slightly under harsh weather. Smeaton thought otherwise. A civil engineer, he planned to try something new. He designed a tower of interlocking stone blocks that fit together the way pieces in a three-dimensional puzzle do. The first stone for the tower weighed two tons (1,814 kg). It was fitted into position in June 1757. In the meantime, Smeaton tinkered with a recipe for a fast-drying waterproof cement. His ideas worked. First lighted in 1759, the lighthouse operated for over a century.

In 1882, when underwater caves began to affect the foundation of Smeaton's tower, officials decided to replace it. Sir James Douglass, a British lighthouse engineer, came up with the design of the final Eddystone tower. His tower used a design much like Smeaton's; it still marks Eddystone Reef. Much of Smeaton's lighthouse was taken apart and moved to Plymouth. It was rebuilt near the harbor, where it stands today.

The triumphs of the Eddystone Lighthouse builders proved that lighthouses could be built in out-of-the-way locations. Hard labor and a good design were critical to completing such a task. At the same time, the demise of each lighthouse demonstrated how fragile the life of a lighthouse, its keepers, and its builders could be. With each new Eddystone Lighthouse, builders learned something that would help people around the world construct better lighthouses.

Longfellow visited still warns boats away from Minot's Ledge.

St. George Reef Lighthouse, California

"Dragon Rocks." That's what an explorer named a dangerous group of rocks off the coast of Northern California. During bad weather, wind and waves combine to create a thick smokelike mist that hides the rocks from mariners. The ledges of St. George Reef, six miles (nearly 10 km) from the town of Crescent City, are no ordinary rocks. They are actually part of a volcanic mountain poking up through the water. These unusual conditions would require an extraordinary lighthouse to warn boats away.

Just as had happened at other locations, a tragic shipwreck made it clear just how much a lighthouse was needed at St. George

St. George Reef Lighthouse workers traveled to the construction site in a cage above the water, as shown in this sketch from the 1884 *Annual Report of the Light-House Board*. *University of Iowa Libraries*

THE STEVENSON FAMILY

Many people enjoy the work of Robert Louis Stevenson, author of *A Child's Garden of Verses* and the adventure stories *Kidnapped* and *Treasure Island*. Today, "Louis" Stevenson is one of Scotland's best-known authors, so it might be hard to believe that his family was disappointed when he became a writer. Instead, his family had expected him to be an engineer like his father, grandfather, and uncles.

Members of the Stevenson family built dozens of lighthouses in Scotland between 1790 and 1940. Robert Louis Stevenson once wrote, "Whenever I smell salt water, I know that I am not far from one of the works of my ancestors." His grandfather, Robert, worked on the famous Bell Rock Lighthouse. Like the Eddystone Lighthouse in England, it was built on a wave-washed rock. Louis's father, Thomas, constructed more than 50 lighthouses. Louis spent three years as an apprentice to learn the engineering trade, but the work did not suit him. When he left to study law, his father was angry. Soon, Louis switched to writing, which he loved. During his career, Louis wrote *Records of a Family of Engineers*. The book included information from family diaries about lighthouse construction. For more information about the Stevenson family of lighthouse builders, visit www.bellrock.org.uk on the Internet.

Reef. In 1865, the *Brother Jonathan* steamer headed north from San Francisco. It wrecked on the rocks during a storm, killing over 150 passengers. Work began on a massive granite lighthouse in 1883 on the reef's Northwest Seal Rock, but it would be nine years before it was lighted for the first time. From the beginning, everyone knew the project would be a challenge, so the government put George Ballantyne in charge of the project. He had overseen construction of a lighthouse at Oregon's Tillamook Rock, another dangerous site.

Unlike at Tillamook Rock, there was no safe place to stay on the reef, so Ballantyne planned to live with his crew aboard a schooner. When the men arrived, they discovered they needed different buoys to moor

Dangerous reefs lurk under the rough waters surrounding the St. George Reef Lighthouse. *U.S. Coast Guard Historian's Office*

made work unbearable. The cage was large enough for six men, and it took about three minutes to travel from the ship to the rock above the frothy seas. When the water was rough, it was impossible to make the journey without getting at least a little wet.

To start, the workers built a concrete and granite base in the shape of an imperfect oval on the rock. This sturdy foundation for the lighthouse building rose 70 feet (21 m) above the water. On top of it, they constructed a massive lighthouse from granite stones. These were not stones like those

that you would throw in a pond, or even large boulders that you might see along a highway. The smallest stone used in the project weighed two-and-a-half tons (over two metric tons). Amazingly, the largest stone weighed 17 tons (over 15 metric tons), or as much as 11 female hippopotamuses! It took over 1,300 stones to complete the expensive project.

St. George Reef cost over $700,000 in 19th-century dollars to construct. Workers kept asking Congress for more money to pay for it. At one point, Congress did not allo-

the boat because the water was deeper than anyone knew. They left in search of larger buoys, and the unoccupied boat broke loose during a storm. At first, everyone assumed the boat had been destroyed. It was later spotted 25 miles (40 km) from the reef, and had to be towed back into position.

The rock was not only impossible to live on; it was also very difficult to land a boat there. For this reason, Ballantyne hooked up a cable from the rock to the mast of the schooner. He attached a cage to the cable, and the men rode the cage back and forth to work. It also gave them a quick way to escape the rock when high winds or waves

Even after the St. George Reef Lighthouse was completed, it was hard to land on the rock. In 1918, an inspector hangs on to a rope as he is hoisted up to the lighthouse. *U.S. Coast Guard Historian's Office*

cate the needed funds, and construction was halted. When you calculate how the value of money has changed over time, the St. George Reef Lighthouse turns out to be the most expensive lighthouse ever built in this country. The sturdy structure has been called "the Mount Everest of lighthouses." The comparison makes sense. After all, like the mountain, the lighthouse towers above its surroundings and looks strong enough to endure for centuries, no matter what the weather. The famous lighthouse appears on a postage stamp released in 2007.

Split Rock Lighthouse, Minnesota

In late November 1905, a fierce storm hit Lake Superior. Twenty-nine ships were damaged or destroyed. Dozens aboard lost their lives. Especially hard hit by the disaster was the flourishing steel industry. Freighters on the lake carried iron ore, a key ingredient needed for producing steel. The ore was mined in northern Minnesota, then shipped eastward to the bustling steel furnaces of Pennsylvania.

After the storm, ship owners lobbied Congress for a lighthouse on the western edge of the lake. "During the last three years considerably over one million dollars' worth of vessels and cargoes have been wrecked in the vicinity of Split Rock Point," they wrote. Bad weather was not the only danger.

The ore itself presented a hazard because its magnetic property skewed compass readings. With an inaccurate compass, ships could easily lose their way.

In the fall of 1909, construction began on Split Rock Lighthouse. The site selected was a sheer cliff 130 feet (40 m) above Lake Superior. Even in the 20th century, construction of the lighthouse was challenging. For starters, just getting to the work site was difficult. Although cars were common in big cities by then, northern Minnesota was still wilderness. There were no roads in the area,

so boats had to transport men and materials to the base of the cliff.

The next challenge was figuring out how to haul heavy building supplies and equipment up to the work site. Workers began by chopping down trees to clear a narrow path uphill through the woods. Somehow, they managed to drag a steam engine mounted on skids up to the work site using ropes and pulleys attached to trees. Imagine the time and brute strength it must have taken to do this backbreaking work without machines. The engine could now

The steel skeleton of the Split Rock Lighthouse takes shape next to the fog signal building during construction. *L. D. Campbell / Minnesota Historical Society*

provide power for a crude wooden derrick, or crane, which had been assembled at the cliff's edge. During construction, the derrick hoisted over 300 tons (272 metric tons) of materials up from supply boats. Concrete workers, brick masons, steel workers, and carpenters all got to the job site by riding in a crate, called a skip, hoisted by the derrick.

The steamer *Red Wing* delivers supplies to the Split Rock Lighthouse construction site in 1909. Note the derrick, or crane, at the top of the cliff, which was used for hauling supplies to the site. *L. D. Campbell / Minnesota Historical Society*

Keepers' houses, fog signal building, and the lighthouse at the Split Rock Light Station, in 1913. In the foreground are rails of a tramway used to deliver goods up the cliff to the station. *U.S. Coast Guard Historian's Office*

To create a level building site on top of the cliff, workers used dynamite to blast away sections of the rock. Engineer Ralph Tinkham recalled the hazards of this work. "One memorable evening I stood in my quarters watching the blasting preparations through the window," he wrote. "When the blast went off, one of the logs covering the blast area, a log of ten inches in diameter and eight feet long, rose into the air and sailed end first . . . down through the open flap entrance of one of the long tents, landing with a crash on the floor between the bunks. Men came scrambling out of the rear end of the tent like ants." Remarkably, no one was hurt.

Once the building site was leveled, the men could construct the lighthouse, homes for the keepers, and other buildings. The octagonal brick lighthouse, which was reinforced with steel, is a popular tourist attraction. Its light no longer shines, except on special occasions.

Chapter Five

The Science Behind Lighthouses

With today's technology, it is simple to operate a lighthouse. So simple, in fact, that people no longer need to live at lighthouses to keep them running. Modern lightbulbs provide a powerful beam that can be seen for miles. Sensors, like those in streetlights, turn lighthouse lights on when it gets dark or stormy.

When daylight comes, or the weather clears, the light shuts off automatically.

A bad storm may inconvenience you when it knocks out power to your house. Lighthouses must shine on no matter what the weather, so back-up power is essential. Emergency generators do this job at some lighthouses. Others rely on solar cells that convert sunlight into electricity, light-emitting diodes, and fuel cells. If a lightbulb burns out while you are reading a good book, you may be frustrated by the interruption. A burned-out bulb at a lighthouse could be more than an inconvenience. It could spell disaster. To prevent outages, modern lighthouses are equipped with automatic bulb changers. When one bulb burns out, an unused bulb rotates into its place automatically.

As you know, lighthouses were a part of the landscape long before the invention of the electric light. So how was it possible to create a bright light without electricity? It wasn't easy. Lighthouse lights evolved slowly as inventors came up with better ways to provide artificial light in homes. Then, in the 19th century, a scientist devised a special lighting system just for lighthouses.

Early Lighting Methods

Before the 1500s, lighthouses relied on the most basic form of man-made light: fire. Controlling an open fire at the top of a lighthouse was difficult. Rain and snow dampened flames. Winds could blow the fire back toward land, making it hard to see. Worse yet, wind gusts could extinguish the fire completely or cause it to spread to the building itself. Hauling wood, coal, or other fuel to the lighthouse site with a cart was a slow process.

Sometime in the 16th century, candles began to replace fires in lighthouses. Builders grouped large candles together in simple chandeliers to make the lights brighter than candles used in nearby homes. This lighting method marked an improvement over open fires, but candles were not ideal. At the time, people used tallow (animal fat) to make candles, which put off an odor. Tallow candles also smoked more than candles we use today, and too much smoke made the light hard to see.

Gradually, people placed different sizes and shapes of reflectors behind candles. Reflectors are part of modern life, although you may not realize it. Take a close look at a flashlight. The shiny silver area that surrounds the lightbulb is a reflector. Formed in the geometric shape called a parabola, this curved area reflects the light from the light source into a single horizontal beam, making the light more intense. Reflectors also concentrate the lights from vehicle headlights.

Lighting in homes and lighthouses improved yet again when oil lamps became popular. Even so, it was hard to create a lighthouse light powerful enough to be seen far away until the late 1700s. That's when a Swiss scientist named Aimé (sometimes spelled Ami) Argand developed a new type of oil lamp. Argand was not interested in the mechanics of providing a light for boaters. Instead, he was looking for a way to improve

the lighting in a distillery he owned. He discovered that a hollow cylindrical wick allowed air to circulate better than an ordinary wick, brightening the flame. After his brother put a broken flask over a flame one day, Argand realized that a protective glass covering would improve his design further. His glass chimney helped cut down on soot, making the light even more intense.

A lighthouse keeper inspects the oil lamps and reflectors in the lantern room. This drawing was published in *Harper's Young People: An Illustrated Weekly* in 1882 to accompany a fictional story about a female lighthouse keeper. *Preus Library, Luther College*

Make a Solar Marshmallow Roaster

You can see how reflectors help concentrate light by making a simple solar marshmallow roaster. You will not produce a marshmallow warm enough to melt chocolate, but it will be mushy inside.

You'll Need

A bright sunny day
Plastic colander, about 12 inches (30.5 cm) in diameter
2 12 × 16-inch (30.5 × 40.6-cm) pieces of aluminum foil
Jumbo marshmallows
Bamboo skewer
2–3 bricks or large rocks, depending on the angle of the sun

Line half the colander with a piece of foil, smoothing it gently to prevent wrinkles.

Crimp around the edge to secure. Use the same method to line the remaining half of the colander with foil.

Slide the marshmallow to the skewer's center.

Position the colander so the sun is directly overhead, propping it up with bricks or rocks for maximum exposure.

To find the best spot for the skewer, place your hand briefly in the bottom of the colander, then raise it slowly until it is a few inches above the colander.

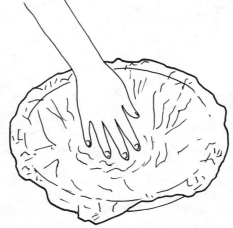

Which spot was warmest? Insert the skewer through the foil and colander holes either vertically or horizontally, so the marshmallow is in the warmest spot.

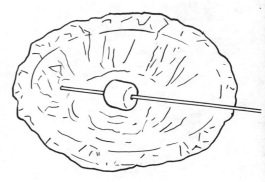

It could take 20 minutes or more to get your marshmallow roasted, depending on where you live, the time of year, and cloud cover. When you can mush the marshmallow easily, remove it from the skewer, and enjoy.

lamp included a reflector that concentrated the light in one beam, and a crude lens designed to magnify the beam. The poorly built lenses were useless, though, and eventually were removed.

A Major Breakthrough

Have you ever studied a straw sitting in a glass of water? Depending on how you look at it, the straw might appear to be cut into two pieces. Of course it really isn't. It just looks that way because of the ability of light to refract, or bend, when it passes from one medium, or substance, to another.

Knowledge about the ability of light to bend played a crucial role in lighthouse history. In 1822, a French scientist named Augustin Fresnel (pronounced Fra-NELL) used his understanding of optics (the science

James Buotte shows off a kerosene lamp similar to one used in 1950 at Burnt Island Lighthouse. Buotte is a guide at the Maine lighthouse, where he himself was a keeper from 1955 to 1958. *Maine Department of Marine Resources*

The Argand lamp was popular in Europe. In 1789, British lighthouses became the first to install these new lighting devices. About 50 British and Irish lighthouses used them by 1820. Argand did not get protection for his invention, and others copied it. One of the imitators was Winslow Lewis of Massachusetts. He sold the patent for his Lewis lamp to the U.S. government in 1812 for use in lighthouses. The Lewis

Fresnel lenses, shown here on display at a fair, were made in a variety of sizes and configurations. *U.S. Coast Guard Historian's Office*

How Does the Liquid Flow?

The fuel used in lighthouse lamps had to flow easily so that it could be soaked up by the wick of the oil lamp. The ease with which liquid flows is called its viscosity. The more easily a liquid flows, the lower its viscosity. You can compare the relative viscosities of two liquids, then determine how temperature affects viscosity.

You'll Need

2 clear 16-ounce (.47-L) plastic shampoo
    bottles (marbles must fit in easily)
Permanent marker
16 ounces (.47 L) each of light corn
    syrup and honey
4 identical small glass marbles
Stopwatch
Sheet of ruled notebook paper
Pencil
Large pot
Ice

Rinse out bottles and remove labels; let dry. Use the marker to draw a horizontal line on each bottle about 1 inch (2.5 cm) from the bottom and 1 inch (2.5 cm) from the top. Fill one bottle with corn syrup, leaving just enough room at the top to drop

a marble in without overflowing. Fill the other bottle just as full with honey.

Place the bottle containing corn syrup on a flat surface. Drop the marble in, and use the stopwatch to time how long it takes the marble to travel between the two lines on the bottle. Record the time on your paper, along with a C next to it.

Drop a second marble in and time its trip. Record the time; then calculate an average by adding the two times together and dividing by two. Repeat the experiment with the bottle of honey. In which liquid did the marble travel faster? Do you think corn syrup or honey has greater viscosity?

Fill the pot with ice. Secure the lid of the bottle of honey; stand in ice for 10 minutes. Remove bottle from ice and repeat experiment. Does it take more or less time for the marble to travel between the lines? Empty the pot and fill with hot water. Submerge the bottle of honey (with lid secure) in it for 5 to 10 minutes. Repeat your experiment. Based on your observation, why do you think lighthouses in some locations used winter oil and summer oil? Which one would have had greater viscosity? Can you figure out where the expression "slower than molasses in January" came from?

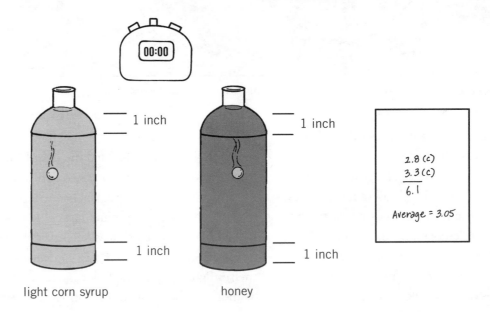

light corn syrup   honey

1 inch
1 inch
1 inch
1 inch

00:00

2.8 (c)
3.3 (c)
6.1

Average = 3.05

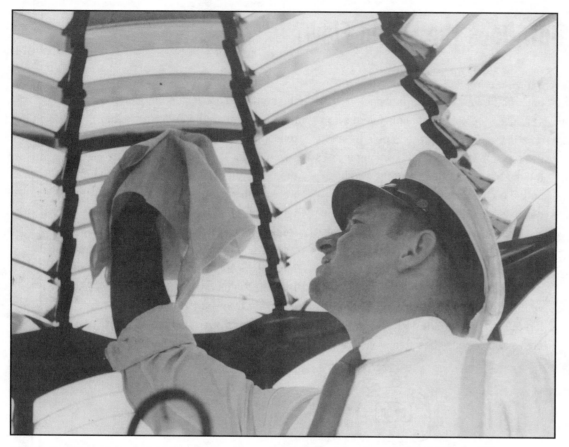

A Coast Guardsman cleans the large Fresnel lens at Boston Lighthouse in the 1950s. *U.S. Coast Guard Historian's Office*

so effective that they could make a light as bright as electric lights would decades later. Some Fresnel lenses still sit atop working lighthouses; others are on display in museums. Fresnel lenses were divided into different orders, or sizes. First-order Fresnel lenses are the largest and provide the brightest lights. They were installed in major lighthouses along an ocean. Fourth-order and smaller lenses were used in lighthouses that marked harbors or piers.

As you hold a cell phone or music player in your palm, it may be hard to comprehend just how large Fresnel lenses had to be to do their job. A first-order lens was approximately eight and one-half feet (2.6 m) tall and weighed nearly 13,000 pounds (5,897 kg)! That's about two feet (.61 m) taller than the average player in the NBA and as heavy as three minivans.

Certainly, the Fresnel lens made the lights in lighthouses much brighter. But the technology offered another huge advantage. Lenses and prisms could be arranged in various ways to make the beams from each lighthouse in a region look different. If all lighthouse beams looked the same, sailors would not be able to use lighthouses to pinpoint their locations. The different beams were possible because Fresnel lenses were available in three main configurations: fixed, flashing, or a combination of fixed and flashing. Fresnel lenses displaying a

of light) to make lighthouses shine brighter than they ever had. His new system was called the Fresnel lens. The name is a bit misleading. When we think of lenses today, we picture the pieces of glass or plastic in eyeglasses, telescopes, or microscopes. A Fresnel lens actually consisted of several magnifying lenses combined with carefully cut pieces of glass called prisms. The prisms

and lenses were mounted in a metal frame in such a way that they directed the light from the lighthouse lamp into one strong beam.

If you picture a giant glass beehive, you have a good idea what many Fresnel lenses looked like. One lighthouse keeper's daughter described the lens as a glass birdcage. In the sunlight, it "glistened like carefully cut diamonds," she recalled. Fresnel lenses were

Bend Light with a Prism

In a Fresnel lens, carefully cut pieces of glass called prisms were arranged so that they would refract, or bend, the light coming from the light source and direct it through magnifying lenses. Some of the glass also reflected light beams. Working together, the prisms directed the light into one continuous beam, greatly increasing the intensity of the lighthouse light. You can see how prisms in the Fresnel lens helped direct light into one beam by using a plastic prism.

Adult supervision required; read and follow laser pointer directions carefully

You'll Need

Plastic prism (from toy or hobby store)
Inexpensive laser pointer (from drug store or office supply store)
Sheet of white computer paper

In a dark room, stand a plastic prism on its end in the middle of the piece of paper on a floor or table. Position laser pointer a few inches away, and shine the laser toward the prism. The beam should be visible on the paper. Observe the direction of the beam as it leaves the prism. What happens to the beam of light if you shine the laser through a different part of the prism?

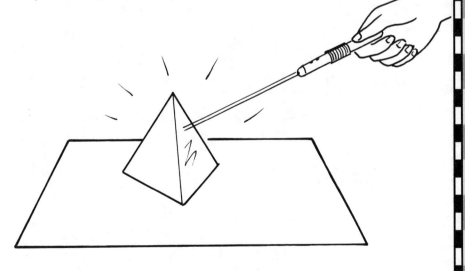

fixed beam did not move. To display a flashing beam or fixed and flashing combination, the entire lens apparatus had to revolve around the light source. In some instances, colored glass was added to the Fresnel lens or lantern room to vary the light's appearance, known as its characteristic.

182.

NOTICE TO MARINERS.

(No. 49, of 1893.)

UNITED STATES OF AMERICA—NORTHERN AND NORTH-WESTERN LAKES.

WHITE FISH POINT LIGHT.

Notice is hereby given that, on or about June 15, 1893, the third order fixed white light at White Fish Point Light Station, southeast part of Lake Superior, Michigan, will be changed to a fixed white light varied by a red flash every 20 seconds. The order of the light will not be changed.

For a few nights immediately preceding the change a fixed white light of a lower order will be exhibited from the tower.

By order of the Light-House Board:

JAMES A. GREER,
Rear-Admiral, U. S. Navy,
Office of the Light-House Board, Chairman.
Washington, D. C., May 10, 1893.

This Notice to Mariners, published by the federal government, explains how the light at the Whitefish Point Lighthouse would change from a fixed characteristic to a fixed white light varied by a red flash. *University of Iowa Libraries*

Investigate How Lighthouses Flashed Long Ago

Today, it is simple to create a flashing light with a switch. When lighthouses relied on Fresnel lenses and oil lamps, lighthouses did not actually flash on and off. Instead, the lamps remained lighted at night and in stormy weather. The appearance of a flash was created when a bull's-eye, or magnifying lens, passed between the sailor and the lighthouse lamp. You can see that effect for yourself with this simple demonstration.

Adult supervision required

You'll Need

Styrofoam craft ring
2 magnifying glasses about 6 inches
    (15.2 cm) tall with straight handles
    (available in office supply stores or
    drugstores).
Pillar candle about 5 inches (12.7 cm)
    tall and matches
Dark room (one with small windows or no
    windows works best)

Place the Styrofoam ring on a flat surface, and press the handle of one magnifying glass anywhere into the foam so that it stands on its own. Turn the ring halfway around, and stick the other magnifying glass in the ring.

Position the candle in the center of the ring. Ask an adult to light the candle; darken the room. Have the adult rotate the ring slowly while you look at a spot on the wall.

Pretend that you are the lighthouse keeper looking out across the sea. The spot represents the position of a ship. Do you see a large spot of light on the wall whenever a lens passes between the wall and the flame? This is similar to the flash created by the bull's-eyes in a Fresnel lens. The lighthouse (the candle) remains on all the time, but it's the flash that is noticeable. Could you change the characteristic of your lighthouse by adding more bull's-eyes (magnifying lenses)? How would the characteristic change if the adult turned the ring more slowly? More quickly?

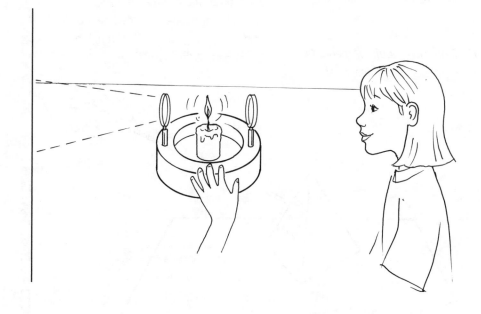

Keeping the Flash Going

You may wonder how people turned the heavy lenses without electric motors. Before electricity, an elaborate clockwork mechanism did the job. The mechanism worked much the way a grandfather clock does. Slowly falling weights provided the propulsion to move a series of gears, which caused the lighthouse lens to turn. The weights usually traveled down a special tube in the lighthouse tower. When the weights descended as far as they could go, the lighthouse keeper had to wind the clockwork mechanism to raise the weights and start the process over. How often the keeper wound the clockwork depended on how tall the lighthouse was and the lens's characteristic. Some keepers had to wind the clockwork every few hours all night long!

Like any machine, the clockwork mechanism sometimes failed. When it did, keepers worked hard to keep the flashing sequence consistent. As a boy, Harry Weeks lived at California's Point Conception Lighthouse where his father was keeper. He later recalled a time when the cable to the clockwork mechanism broke. The keepers' only alternative was to turn the lens by hand for over two hours. To maintain the correct flashing pattern, keepers used a stopwatch to time the rotations. "There were sixteen sides, or flash panels, and the char-

 ## SEARCHING FOR THE BEST FUEL

If you have been to a lighthouse, you might have noticed a small building called an oil house. It may even have been part of a visitors' center or gift shop. In the United States, oil houses were built in the late 1800s for the safe storage of mineral oil. Today, we refer to that type of lamp oil as kerosene. At the time, kerosene was the primary fuel used in the oil lamps that created the light in lighthouses. Because the oil ignited easily, the government erected sturdy buildings for storing it away from the keeper's house and lighthouse. Keepers poured the kerosene from large containers into brass cans that they hauled up the lighthouse stairs.

U.S. lighthouses began to use kerosene in 1877. When kerosene burned, it did not create as much smoke as other oils, which made it popular for use in lighthouses. By 1885, it was the primary fuel used in lighthouses in this country. What did people use before kerosene? Sperm oil from whales was the primary fuel for many years until the price rose sharply in the mid-1800s. Colza oil (from cabbages) and lard oil (from animal fat) were used, too.

Keepers have tried other fuels over the years. In the early 1800s, porpoise oil was tested in North Carolina, but it did not work as well as sperm oil. A lighthouse in Barcelona, New York, used natural gas for a time. In Canada, a lighthouse on an island with lots of seals relied on seal oil, and a lighthouse in South Africa once used oil made from the tails of sheep.

acteristic was a flash every thirty seconds, so the lens made a complete rotation every eight minutes," Weeks recalled.

Getting Fresnel lenses to rotate at the right speed was critical for creating just the right light characteristic. Friction, however, slowed the speed of rotation. Friction is the property that makes two objects resist moving across each other. To make the lenses turn more easily, they were mounted on

Discover the Benefits of Ball Bearings

The following demonstration will let you see how ball bearings work.

You'll Need

10-inch (25.4-cm) bamboo skewer or wooden chopstick

Ruler

Pencil

Plastic lid that fits over top of can (a peanut butter jar lid works well)

Packaging tape (about two inches square)

Small (10–11-ounce) (.25 L) can of unopened soup

6 small glass marbles

One teaspoon vegetable oil

Mark the midpoint of the skewer. Center the skewer on the top of the plastic lid and secure with tape. Place the lid on top of the can. With an index finger, gently push the stick, with just enough power to spin the lid. (Spin it too fast, and the lid

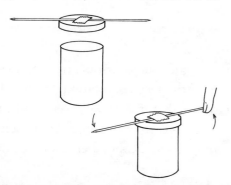

will fall off.) Notice the level of resistance when you spin the lid.

Remove the lid and place six marbles on top of the can.

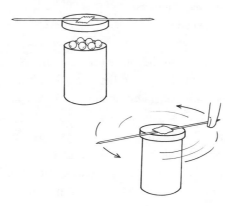

Replace the lid and spin the stick as you did before. Was it easier to turn the lid? It should have been. The marbles have a smaller surface area that touches the can than the lid did. The marbles act like bearings to reduce friction between the can and lid.

Remove the lid and marbles. Pour oil on top of the can, and coat the marbles in it. Put the lid back on top of the marbles and can, and spin it again. Did the lid spin more quickly or slowly? Why do you think lighthouse keepers had to oil ball bearings regularly? Do you think using a thicker liquid, such as honey, would make it harder or easier to spin the lid?

Captain E. J. Moore, keeper of the Grosse Point Lighthouse in Illinois from 1889 until 1922, winds the clockwork mechanism. *Donald J. Terras / Grosse Point Lighthouse National Landmark*

huge metal balls called ball bearings. The balls reduced friction, allowing the lenses to turn faster.

While ball bearings helped Fresnel lenses turn, they also had drawbacks. For starters, they required a lot of maintenance. In addition, as the number of lighthouses increased, people needed to turn lenses faster than bearings allowed. By revolving lenses faster, more and different flash patterns could be developed. Toward the end of the 19th century, lens manufacturers began to float some Fresnel lenses in mercury. Thanks to the mercury float, a huge lens could be made to revolve quickly with just the touch of a finger. Mercury remains a liquid at a wide range of temperatures, meaning it would not freeze in cold climates.

A close-up view of a clockwork mechanism with the ball bearings visible, from the 1899 *Annual Report of the Light-House Board. University of Iowa Libraries*

Beyond Ball Bearings: Floating a Heavy Lens

You can't experiment with mercury because it's a poisonous chemical. Even today, no one knows for sure how it affected keepers who had to work close to it. With this experiment, you can learn about density by comparing the densities of everyday liquids.

You'll Need

Notebook paper
Pencil
Four disposable cups, at least 4 ounces (.19 L)
Measuring cup
3 ounces (.09 L) each of water, oil, maple syrup, and molasses
4 each of various small objects, such as paper clips, almonds, marbles, and raisins

Make a simple chart on the paper by writing the names of the four liquids across the top of the page. Write the names of the objects down the length of the page.

Pour three ounces of the liquids into different cups. (Be sure to wash the measuring cup between pourings.) Drop a raisin into each cup. Do you think it will float or sink? Record your results by writing an "F" for float and an "S" for sink on your chart in the appropriate space. Were your guesses correct? Drop the remaining objects into each liquid and record your results.

Did a marble float in any of the liquids? What about the almond? Were you surprised that you could get certain objects to float in one or more of the liquids? Based on your observations, which liquid appears to be the densest?

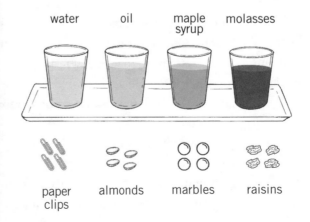

The Twin Lights of Navesink in modern times. Built in 1862, these towers replaced the twin lights where the first Fresnel lenses in this country were installed. *U.S. Coast Guard Historian's Office*

Lens manufacturers also chose mercury because only a small amount was needed, and there wasn't much room at the top of a lighthouse. To get a first-order lens to float in mercury, you could use less than 2 percent of the volume needed to get it to float in water. Why? Mercury is very dense, or heavy, when compared to water.

Putting the Fresnel Lens to Work

The first Fresnel lens in the world was installed at Cordouan Lighthouse in France in 1823. The new technology was an instant success, and Europeans moved quickly to install the Fresnel lens in their lighthouses. The United States did not. Penny-pinching Stephen Pleasonton, head of the U.S. lighthouse system, thought the Fresnel lens was too expensive. He also boasted that the cheaper Lewis lamp and reflector system was just as effective.

Sea captains and others disagreed. Critics declared that U.S. lighthouses "are greatly inferior in brilliancy" to those in Europe. Pleasonton said these charges were

"entirely unfounded." Perhaps he wanted to remain loyal to Lewis, who also built many lighthouses for the U.S. government. Lewis and Pleasonton became friends, and Lewis's knowledge of sailing and construction helped Pleasonton do his job.

It took action by Congress to force a change. In 1841, two Fresnel lenses were installed at the twin lights at Navesink, New Jersey. Afterward, the captain of a mail steamer commented, "The Navesink lights are by far the best on our coast which have come under my observation, particularly the revolving light, which can be seen twenty-five miles."

In the 1850s, officials recommended that all U.S. lighthouses use the Fresnel lens. The changeover took place rapidly. Workers rebuilt and enlarged the lantern rooms at many lighthouses to accommodate the big lenses. In some cases, builders had to make existing lighthouses taller so that the more powerful beam would be visible farther away.

Electricity provided power to a few lighthouses in the 1880s, but it would be several more decades before it reached the most remote light stations. In the early 1900s, an explosive gas called acetylene gas became popular for use in lighthouses and buoys. Then, someone developed a way to make lights generated by kerosene brighter using an incandescent oil vapor lamp, or IOV. Today's camping lanterns work on the same principle.

Philmore Wass liked to help his father with the IOV lamp on Libby Island in Maine. "Kerosene for the light had to be carried from a storage building about a hundred feet away," he later wrote. "The hard part was carrying it up the spiral staircase to the top of the tower. Another time-consuming job was pumping air into the pressure tank. The kerosene was sprayed, under pressure, through a jet. The vaporized fuel, when burned, heated the mantle, which glowed with an intense white light." It was a shock to see such a bright light when the light first came on. "Somewhat blinded, we would carefully make our way down the stairs, hanging onto a rope attached to rings in the wall," he recalled.

Technology Takes Over

Running lighthouses was important work, but there were drawbacks. Paying a keeper to live at a lighthouse cost a lot of money. Depending on the location, keepers risked their lives living at a lighthouse, or simply getting there. There were two basic solutions to these problems. People could find ways to replace lighthouses, or they could invent ways to let lighthouses run by themselves. They did both.

In the second half of the 1800s, buoys became larger and more complex. Buoys had started out as small floating devices to mark

Keeper Fannie Salter displays the small lightbulb inside the fourth-order Fresnel lens at the Turkey Point Lighthouse. *U.S. Coast Guard Historian's Office*

harbors. Gradually, bells were added to them, then whistles and lights. Eventually, buoys could emit radio signals that helped boaters determine their location. With all these additions, large buoys were just as effective as some lighthouses. They were also simpler, cheaper, and safer to operate. In the 20th century, a variety of electronic aids began to help sailors, such as radar.

More recently, global positioning systems have made it possible for boaters to determine their precise location without the aid of a lighthouse.

In areas where buoys did not take over, the search was on to let machines do the work of running a lighthouse. Finding a way to turn a light on and off without electricity, though, was more complex than simply

67

Keeper Elson Small takes time out from his duties at Maine's St. Croix River Lighthouse to milk a cow in the mid-1940s. The lighthouse has since been destroyed by fire. *U.S. Coast Guard Historian's Office*

mooring a buoy. In the early 1900s, Swedish scientist Gustaf Dalén became a pioneer in devising ways to use acetylene gas in lighting. His inventions helped make the gas practical and economical for use in lighthouses. His sun valve changed the way lighthouses around the world operated.

The sun valve consisted of four rods enclosed in glass. A black rod was surrounded by three metallic rods, which helped reflect light onto the black one. When the sun came up, the black rod warmed and grew slightly larger. Its expansion triggered a device that shut off the gas supply in the lighthouse. The lack of sunlight at night caused the black rod to contract. By doing so, gas could flow freely, turning the lighthouse light on. In 1912, Dalén received the Nobel Prize in physics for his work on lighthouses and buoys.

As electricity reached more lighthouses, lightbulbs replaced sun valves and IOV lamps. Switches made a keeper's job easier; automatic bulb changers and timers helped make keepers obsolete. Lightbulbs were used with Fresnel lenses, instead of oil lamps. The glass lenses, though, were no longer essential to creating a powerful light. Gradually, aerobeacons replaced some lenses. Aerobeacons held a bulb and a reflector, much like flashlights, and were weather resistant. They had been developed to provide powerful lights at airports that could be used outside no matter what the weather. Modern plastic lenses were even more effective at providing lights for boaters. Both aerobeacons and modern lenses could be mounted on a post or skeletal tower. A lighthouse tower with an enclosed lantern room was not essential anymore. Some historic lighthouses still display Fresnel lenses, but most do not.

Chapter Six

Keep the Lights Burning!
The Job of the Keeper

Keeper Samuel Burgess was worried—and with good reason. The supply boat hadn't visited remote Matinicus Rock, Maine, in September as scheduled. It was January 1856, and his family was running low on provisions. Burgess, who tended the twin lights on the treeless island in Penobscot Bay, feared winter storms would trap the family without enough food. His only son had left months earlier to work on a fishing boat in Canada. His invalid wife and four daughters remained. It was up to Keeper Burgess to make the dangerous boat trip over 20 miles (32 km) to shore for supplies.

The experienced keeper surely realized that unpredictable weather might keep him ashore a few extra days. Luckily, he knew he could depend on his oldest daughter to take care of the family and the lighthouse. Seventeen-year-old Abbie had assisted her father with lighthouse chores since the family had moved to the island about three years earlier. Before Keeper Burgess left, he is believed to have said, "I can depend on you, Abbie."

This was not the first time Abbie had taken on such big responsibilities. Keeper Burgess often went to the mainland to sell lobsters to earn extra money. The keeper's daughter knew how dangerous the season's winter gales could be. She had read the January 1839 entry in the logbook left by a former keeper. It read, "Lighthouse tore down by the sea." The keeper had survived, and two days later, he lit a temporary beacon. Sturdier towers now stood on the island, along with the Burgess family's stone house.

Shortly after Keeper Burgess left, the wind direction changed. Abbie knew this meant a big storm might be approaching. For the next few days, the waves grew bigger and bigger. As conditions worsened, Abbie realized the family's hens were in danger. She could not bear to watch the birds drown without trying to save them. After all, the hens were valued companions that made life on the island a little less lonely. They also supplied much-needed fresh eggs.

Her mother warned her not to dare a risky rescue, but Abbie was determined. When the waves subsided briefly, Abbie ran outside with a basket into knee-deep water. (It could not have been easy for her to move quickly, since women and girls wore long dresses or skirts at the time.) Despite her confining wardrobe, Abbie managed to rescue all but one of the birds. As soon as she got back to the house, a huge wave came up and covered the island. The hens were safe and so was she—at least for the time being.

These twin lighthouses on Matinicus Rock, Maine, were built in 1857, to replace an earlier set of twin lights. *U.S. Coast Guard Historian's Office*

Tend an Oil Lamp

Before electricity, lighthouse keepers had to tend oil lamps. This time-consuming task involved carefully measuring out the oil and carrying it up the lighthouse stairs. If the lamp smoked, keepers had to clean the lamp chimney often. The burned part of the wick had to be trimmed. With help from an adult, you can learn how an oil lamp works and find out about the hard part of keeping the lights burning.

Adult supervision required. Never leave an oil lamp unattended.

You'll Need

Inexpensive decorative oil lamp (available in hardware stores or the housewares section of larger stores, or ask family friends if they have one you could borrow)
Lamp oil
Matches
Scissors

Remove the chimney and burner (the part with the wick attached) from the lamp. Ask an adult to help you fill the lamp with oil according to directions from the lamp man-

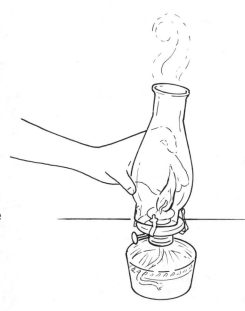

ufacturer. Replace the burner for about 15 minutes to allow the wick to absorb the oil. (A wick absorbs oil like a paper towel absorbs spills; only more slowly.) Turn the knob to adjust the wick according to the manufacturer's directions, or usually just above the hole in the burner where the wick protrudes.

Ask an adult to light the wick. Replace the chimney with the help of an adult. (The chimney can get hot fast, so move quickly to prevent burns.) With adult supervision, raise the height of the wick until the flame produces a little smoke. After the smoky flame produces soot on the chimney, lower the wick to its normal level.

When you are done, have an adult blow out the flame. When the chimney cools, remove it from the lamp. Did the soot create a stain that needs cleaning? If so, run it under warm soapy water, then let it dry. Is the wick slightly charred? If so, trim the wick after it cools by using scissors to cut off the charred part. Rinse and dry the scissors before putting away.

Wash your hands after using. Always store the lamp and oil according to the directions. Your family might want to use the oil lamp when your electricity goes out.

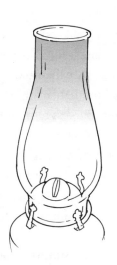

At one point during the storm, large waves slammed against the house and flooded the dwelling. Fearing for her family's safety, Abbie moved everyone into one of the tall, sturdy light towers. She later wrote to a friend, "As the tide came in, the sea rose higher and higher, till the only endurable places were the light-towers. If they stood we were saved, otherwise our fate was only too certain."

Despite these obstacles, Abbie remained strong. Every evening at sunset, she carried whale oil up the stairs of each tower to the lantern room, where she lit the lamps. She stayed up much of the night to make sure the lamps burned brightly, trimming, or removing, the already burned sections of the wick when necessary to keep the flame strong. At sunrise, she extinguished the lamps by lowering the wick. For four weeks, she took care of her family and the island's lighthouses. "Though at times greatly exhausted with my labors, not once did the lights fail," she wrote. When Keeper Burgess returned, he thanked Abbie, who became famous along the Maine coast for her heroism.

Abbie was not the only hard-working family member of a lighthouse keeper. Keepers knew they could lose their jobs if the light went out during the night, regardless of the reason. As a result, they often trained their children and spouses to tend the light in case of an emergency.

Abbie Burgess. *U.S. Coast Guard Historian's Office*

Throughout history, there are many examples of sick or injured keepers leaving their posts while a family member kept the light burning.

A Beacon to Sailors

The main duty of the lighthouse keeper was to keep the light on all night and in bad weather. For a long time, tending the light meant keepers got little sleep. When light-

houses used oil lamps, keepers stayed up at night to make sure the flames did not go out. (Vents in the lantern room let out smoke from the lamps, but also let in drafts that could blow out the flames.) Cold temperatures in the unheated lighthouses thickened some types of oil. When the oil congealed, the wicks of the lighthouse lamps could not absorb it adequately, causing the flames to dim or go out. Sometimes keepers had to descend the tower stairs to heat up the oil so it could flow properly. The more lamps the lighthouse had, the more work there was to do.

Keepers also carefully trimmed the already burned parts of the wick, giving them the nickname "wickies." Directions written in 1838 instructed keepers in the United States to trim the wicks every four hours throughout the night. In the early years of the lighthouse system, each lamp often had more than one wick, making the trimming process time-consuming. At lighthouses with more than one keeper, each keeper was in charge for part of the night. The hours from dusk to dawn were split into shifts, or periods called "watches." One watch might last from 8:00 P.M. until midnight, while the next one would run from midnight until 4:00 A.M. This system allowed each keeper to get a little sleep.

Keeping the glass windows of the lantern room clean was a key to making the

The government supplied lighthouse keepers, such as Elmer Byrnes of the Point Iroquois Lighthouse in Michigan, with detailed instructions. *U.S. Forest Service*

light visible. In good weather, this was not a problem. During storms, snow and ice had to be scraped from the windows. Sometimes debris would even smash the glass. That's what happened during a storm at Tillamook Rock Lighthouse in Oregon. In October 1934, rocks weighing as much as 60 pounds

MADAM KEEPER

Many people are surprised to learn that women worked as lighthouse keepers long before most women had careers. Hannah Thomas is recognized as the first female keeper in the country. She kept the lighthouse at Plymouth, Massachusetts, beginning around 1776. Female keepers usually learned how to keep the light from their husbands or fathers. When a male keeper died or became too sick to work, his wife or daughter often applied for the job. Frequently, but not always, a female family member received an appointment.

In the first part of the 1800s, lighthouse official Stephen Pleasonton believed that widows should replace keepers as long as they were "steady and respectable." Why? Because it was "so necessary" that a light be "in the hands of experienced keepers," he wrote. In the 1920s, the government decided that women were no longer suited for the job. Newer machines were more complicated to operate. (At the time, women were not expected to understand machines.) The equipment also required more muscle power, and people did not think females

were up to the job. Despite this thinking, female keepers were allowed to stay on the job; they just stopped receiving new appointments.

For much of the 20th century, only men could join the Coast Guard, so after the U.S. Coast Guard took over the lighthouse system in 1939, there were no female Coast Guard keepers. That changed in 1980, when a female Coast Guard member was assigned to the New Dungeness Lighthouse in Washington State.

Fannie Salter, keeper of the Turkey Point Lighthouse in Maryland, and her son feed turkeys at the station in 1931. Salter was keeper at the station for over 20 years, from 1925 until 1947. *R. C. Smith / U.S. Coast Guard Historian's Office*

(27 kg) landed in the lantern room. This was no small feat since the top of the lighthouse stood 133 feet (40.5 m) above normal high water!

During spring and fall migration, birds presented a big problem at some lighthouses. Drawn to the light, they headed directly for the lantern room windows; large birds could shatter the glass. Keeper W. W. Wells recalls a time when the sound of birds flying into the lantern glass surprised the men at Maine's Saddleback Ledge Lighthouse. "We keepers were setting in the kitchen talking about the World War [World War I] when bang, bang, bang, something came against the window panes," he said. "We thought that another war had started that we had not heard about. All at once I heard glass smash in the lantern and with this I thought sure the enemy was trying to extinguish the light." More than 120 birds (most of them dead) ended up at the base of the tower. Cleaning bird feathers and guts off the lantern room glass was a messy job. Dead birds provided one benefit, though: a meal of fresh duck or goose.

Battling the Weather

Bad weather did not simply make it harder for keepers to do their jobs. It could endanger their well-being. Harriet Colfax had to make her way along a narrow pier to reach the light at Michigan City, Indiana. Despite an elevated walkway, called a catwalk, high waves could turn this seemingly simple task into a hair-raising one. On September 18, 1872, she recorded that high waves "very nearly" carried her into the lake. Less than two weeks later, she wrote, "went to the beacon tonight with considerable risk of life."

Like Harriet Colfax, Keeper James H. Wiest was lucky to survive his time tending a light. In the summer of 1914, Keeper Wiest was struck by lightning while on duty at New York's Danskammer Point Lighthouse. As the tallest buildings in an area, lighthouses were prone to lightning strikes. The lightning darted in through the window and hit Wiest, knocking him from his chair and paralyzing him briefly. Even so, he stayed at his post all night. When a doctor examined him the next morning, he found a "broad streak reaching from under my right arm, down my right side and leg to the ankle," the keeper wrote in a report. "The bolt passed from me to and through the floor."

In January 1877, it was bitterly cold along the Chesapeake Bay, near Maryland and Virginia. Because of the freezing weather, huge chunks of floating ice became stuck against Maryland's Hooper Strait Lighthouse. After a while, the pressure became too strong for the screw pile lighthouse, which stood in the bay one mile (1.6 km) from shore. The building's iron supports gave way, and the lighthouse sank quickly.

Keeper John Cornwall and his assistant scrambled to get out. There was no time to save government property or their belongings. Somehow, the keepers managed to climb into one of the station's boats, which they began to pull along the ice. With no way to contact anyone, they could only wait and hope that someone would rescue them. About 24 hours later, the resident of an island in the bay did just that. The keepers suffered from frostbite but were OK otherwise. The outcome of the lighthouse building was not as favorable: it ended up floating several miles down the bay. Days later, the government salvaged some equipment, but the building itself was ruined.

These men were lucky. Hurricanes and other storms could trap keepers and their families at or near lighthouses, sometimes with tragic results. That is what happened in New England on a horrible day in 1938. On September 21, a huge hurricane hit the region. One victim was the daughter of the keeper at the Beavertail Lighthouse on Rhode Island's Jamestown Island. Marion Chellis was riding home from school on a bus when rising waters stalled the vehicle. The students managed to escape, but young Marion could not hold on to her 11-year-old brother's hand as water swirled around them. She drowned, along with several

Less than half an hour later, a shorter, but stronger quake struck. No one could have predicted what would happen next. At 2:18 A.M., the men at the Radio Direction Finder Station heard a terrible roar. Without warning, a massive wall of water struck the Coast Guard buildings. This tsunami, or seismic wave, had been caused by an undersea landslide. It may have been as tall as 100 feet (30 m); tsunamis can travel at speeds up to 500 miles per hour (800 kilometers per hour). The men at the RDF station survived the powerful wave, but the lighthouse did not. The seemingly sturdy structure was destroyed. At 7:00 A.M., the grim search through debris began. All the keepers died, but only one body could be identified.

The Scotch Cap Lighthouse before the tsunami (left), and the destruction afterward (right). *U.S. Coast Guard Historian's Office*

other children on the bus that day. The storm also claimed the lives of family members at other lighthouses.

Even the most modern building methods proved no match for Mother Nature. During the night of April 1, 1946, four Coast Guardsmen were asleep at Alaska's Scotch Cap Light Station. A fifth man stood watch. Located on Unimak Island in northern Alaska, the white, five-story lighthouse had been built six years earlier of reinforced concrete. Close to 1:30 A.M., an earthquake lasting about 30 seconds rocked the area. Coast Guardsmen stationed just up the hill at a Radio Direction Finder Station telephoned the keepers. The men living in the lighthouse said they were "plenty scared," but they stayed on the job.

To the Rescue!

On a very windy day in 1914, the *Ora Endress* boat capsized in high winds near the Whitefish Point (Michigan) Light Station. Despite large waves, keeper Robert Carlson rowed out to the wreck with two fishermen and rescued the 11 passengers onboard. One of the rescued men wrote later, "There is not one man in a thousand who would have attempted to launch a small boat in such a

Lighthouse keeper Ida Lewis was so famous that she appeared on the front page of *Harper's Weekly* in July 1869. *University of Iowa Libraries Special Collections & University Archives*

sea, and few men who could handle a boat at all in such a wind with the seas running high." Although the victim may have been right about how rare Carlson's bravery was among most people, his actions were not unusual among lighthouse keepers. Keepers were directed to "aid wrecked persons as far as lies in their power," and they took this duty seriously.

Strong men were not the only ones to attempt daring rescues. When 14-year-old Maebelle Mason spotted a man whose boat had capsized in the Detroit River, she set out to rescue him. Her father, Orlo Mason, keeper of the Mamajuda Lighthouse, was away at the time. Maebelle managed to launch a boat and row more than one mile (1.6 km) each way to save the boater. Her hard work and bravery earned her many awards, including the rare Silver Lifesaving Medal.

The life-saving skills of two petite female keepers are legendary. Ida Lewis of Newport, Rhode Island, received credit for rescuing four careless teenagers, young sailors, and even a sheep. In 1869, a newspaper wrote that her rescue of a man "was a most daring feat, and required courage and perseverance such as few of the male sex even are possessed of."

Like Ida, Kate Walker of New York City did not fit anyone's image of a powerful rescuer. The keeper of the Robbins Reef, New York, lighthouse stood less than five feet (1.5 m) tall and weighed about 100 pounds (45 kg). She was described as having "shrewd gray eyes" and skin "as ruddy as a sea captain's." As keeper of the lighthouse near Staten Island for over 30 years, Kate rescued more than 50 people.

The rescue that stood out most in her mind, though, was that of a dog. One cold,

Keeper Kate Walker is shown here in a photo that accompanied an article about her in *Harper's Weekly* in 1909. *University of Iowa Libraries Special Collections & University Archives*

windy day in March, a schooner became stuck on the reef near the lighthouse. Quickly, Kate launched a boat and rowed toward the disabled ship. As her small boat lurched in the waves, she managed to rescue all five sailors. Kate was preparing to return to the lighthouse, when one of the men called out to his shaggy brown dog, named Scotty. Kate used an oar to lift the drenched pooch out of the wind-whipped water. The trip back to the lighthouse required courage and strength. It took Kate two hours to reach her little round home. When she got to the lighthouse, she climbed the tall, straight ladder leading into her home with Scotty in her arms.

The weary dog fell over in Kate's warm kitchen. Concerned, Kate placed Scotty on the cushion of a rocking chair and covered him with a blanket. To revive the pet, she forced hot coffee down his throat. After the sailors left Scotty behind so that they could go ashore, the little dog followed Kate everywhere. When the ship's captain returned to pick up the dog after three days, Scotty whined, and Kate noticed tears in his eyes. She told a writer, "Then I learned that dogs really weep. . . . It is strange that one of the pleasantest memories I have of my thirty-two years in the lighthouse should be of the loving gratitude of a dog."

Fog as Thick as Pea Soup

In some locations, troublesome fog could render a light from a lighthouse useless. In these places, keepers had the extra job of operating a fog signal. When Mazie Freeman was a little girl, she mistakenly thought her father turned on the fog signal at Petit Manan Lighthouse to chase away the fog. Her dad finally explained that the loud noise could not get rid of the fog. It only warned ships away from the island's shore.

Keepers had to operate the fog signal day and night as long as the fog lasted. In some places, this could be days at a time. Figuring out when to turn on the fog signal was a low-tech operation. When keepers could no longer see certain landmarks, such as a nearby island, they got the fog signal going. For a long time, it took much time

and effort to operate fog signals. The first fog signal used in the United States was a cannon. The keeper at Boston Light fired it in response to cannon fire from ships. Cannons were awkward, dangerous, and time-consuming to operate. Because it took time to reload the guns, it was impossible to issue sounds at frequent intervals. Next

Sailor the dog liked to ring the fog bell at Wood Island Lighthouse in Maine, in response to greetings that ships tooted. Sailor is shown with Thomas Henry Orcutt, who was keeper at the light from 1886 until 1905. *Roderick Jeffers*

The fog bell at the Ediz Hook Lighthouse in Washington State weighed nearly 4,000 pounds. It was housed in a bell tower and rung automatically. *U.S. Coast Guard Historian's Office*

her friend Margaret behind at Maryland's Drum Point Lighthouse. When fog developed on the Chesapeake Bay, Myrtle attempted to get the automatic fog-bell striker going. When it failed to work, she and her friend rang a bell by hand until Myrtle's parents returned. "It took the two of us to ring it: 'one, two, three, ring!'" Margaret recalled as an adult.

The sound of bells did not always travel far enough to help sailors, especially when the surf was loud. In the second half of the 19th century, people tried out several new types of fog signals. A Connecticut man named Celadon Daboll combined a large trumpet to amplify sound with a reed like those used in wind instruments, such as the clarinet. The trumpet resembled a cheerleader's megaphone. Compressed air powered the signal. (You use compressed air when you sound a bicycle horn or blow up the tire on your bicycle.) A person could use a hand pump to power the signal, or a horse could operate a machine that generated the air. Daboll's signal was not adopted widely because it was difficult to operate. His idea to use a machine to power a fog signal had merit, however. Even after other machines began to power fog signals, his trumpets were used to help amplify their sounds.

Steam-generated fog signals began to make their debut in the late 1850s. Running

came fog bells, which had to be rung by hand for decades, leaving keepers with aching arms and little time to sleep.

Even after mechanical bells were developed in the mid-1800s, keepers had to wind the clockwork and maintain the equipment. When the machinery broke, keepers resorted to clanging the bells by hand. One day in 1923, Keeper Cale Stowe and his wife left their teenage daughter, Myrtle, and a steam engine was a lot of work, so the Lighthouse Service often assigned an extra keeper to stations with these signals. "The old fog signal building was like a miniature factory," recalled Bertha Endress. She lived at the Whitefish Point, Michigan, Lighthouse, where her grandfather was a keeper, in the early 1900s. "You had to yell to make yourself heard," she recalled. "It was hot. During a foggy spell, one boiler was fired up to make steam to blow the foghorn. The other boiler was set up and ready to be fired in case the first ceased to function which did happen now and then." It could take 30 to 45 minutes to generate the necessary steam; sometimes the fog disappeared just as

Lee Benton, assistant keeper at Split Rock Lighthouse in Minnesota, with the gasoline air compressors that powered the fog signals. He is standing in the fog signal building about 1911. *National Park Service—Apostle Islands National Lakeshore*

CREATIVE USES FOR FOG SIGNALS

At Ballast Point Lighthouse in California, the Engel family found a new use for the station's fog signal. Norma Engel and her brothers liked to coax visiting friends to place their heads inside the large fog bell. One of the Engel children would then strike the bell, stunning the unsuspecting friend. "For the rest of the day, anyone who lent himself to this form of medieval torture, roamed around with a very strange look," she recalled. Lighthouse officials certainly would not have approved of this prank, but they probably never knew about it.

In northern Michigan, the Byrnes family at the Point Iroquois Lighthouse found a more practical use for the fog signal. In the days before indoor plumbing, the children had to take baths in a tub placed in front of the kitchen stove. When the weather was warm and foggy, they walked outside to the fog signal building instead. There, they took a shower hooked up by their father using water heated by the steam engine that powered the signal!

the frustrated keepers got the engines in full operation.

At the beginning of the 20th century, another innovation changed the way sailors received warnings in the fog. A Canadian named J. P. Northey received a patent for a diaphone fog signal. (Diaphone means two sounds.) At first, the machine was powered by compressed air. Later, diesel engines and electric motors provided power to operate the signal. The unique sound of the dia-phone evolved over time. It is best known for producing a low groan that sounds a bit like "BEEEEEEOHH." (In fact, a soap company used the sound in commercials at one point to convey that their product could get rid of body odor, or B.O.)

Everyday Maintenance

You might think that keepers had plenty of spare time after the light was shut off at

Lighthouse keepers had to polish a lot of brass, including brass tools. These brass items—a lamp oiler, oil measuring pitcher, and funnel—were placed on a drip tray that collected spilled oil for reuse. *Michigan Lighthouse Conservancy*

Cleaning brass was such an unpopular job that a poem was written about it. The author was Fred Morong, who traveled to lighthouses making repairs in the early 1900s. One verse of the poem read, "The devil himself could never invent / A material causing more worldwide lament / And in Uncle Sam's service about ninety per cent / Is Brasswork."

Plenty of other materials besides brass needed cleaning and care. Before lighthouses ran by electricity, keepers polished the lamps' reflectors during the day so that they would reflect as much light as possible at night. They also had to clean the smoke and soot off the lamps' glass chimneys and lantern room windows. Whale oil caused the lamps to smoke a lot; the change to kerosene reduced this work. Once the Fresnel lens system was installed, keepers cleaned and polished each of the lens' many prisms using a special cloth so that they did not scratch the delicate glass. They also tested the flashing sequence regularly, oiled machinery, and kept detailed records.

Keepers also had to make sure the grounds around the lighthouse were tidy by mowing the grass, trimming trees, and car-

dawn. In fact, they had many other chores. One of the jobs keepers and their families did during the day was clean brass. Brass, a metal made from copper and zinc, had to be cleaned regularly so that it would shine like gold. Exposure to air continually tarnished brass or turned it brown and dull. The job seemed never-ending because so many things at a lighthouse were brass: oil lamps, tools, doorknobs, railings, dustpans, even the frame for the Fresnel lens. "You had to keep the brass clean so it wouldn't corrode," recalls Wilbur York, whose father was a lighthouse keeper. "Someone would put a hand on it, and it'd have to be polished all over again."

It is likely that these keepers' children at the Long Point Lighthouse in Massachusetts polished brass to help their parents. This photo was taken before 1875, when the lighthouse was replaced by a square tower. *U.S. Coast Guard Historian's Office*

Make and Test Your Own Brass Polish

Acidic materials such as lemon juice can be used to make an effective brass cleaner. After you try out this recipe, you will understand the comments of one lighthouse keeper in Alaska. In 1946, when bad weather left the Cape Spencer Lighthouse low on supplies, Keeper Paul Reager joked, "I once made a lemon pie out of brass polish, which was high in citric acid. Made a darn good pie, too."

You'll Need

Small mixing bowl
2 tablespoons baking soda
1 tablespoon lemon juice
Spoon
Paper towels

12-inch (30.5-cm) brass rod, about ½-inch (1.3-cm) in diameter (available in model building section at hobby stores, craft stores and hardware stores). Pick the dirtiest-looking one you can find.

Place baking soda in bowl. Add lemon juice and mix with spoon.

Dip a paper towel in the mixture, making sure that some of the polish adheres to the towel. Rub the paper towel, polish side down, back and forth along the rod. After a minute or so, you should see some of the tarnish on the paper towel.

Rinse the rod off under warm water to check your progress. Re-apply polish to another paper towel (unless there is still some on the first one) and keep polishing. Do you like polishing brass? Why or why not? Would you want it to be one of your regular chores? How would you feel if an inspector checked your work?

ing for plants. Some cut and hauled firewood to heat their homes or provide fuel for engines that powered fog signals. They also made minor repairs around the station. "If you were on an offshore station and something went wrong, you couldn't very well call a plumber or electrician," recalled longtime keeper Frank Schubert. "You had to either do it yourself or do without."

Charles Jennings, keeper of the Lovell's Island Range Lights in Boston Harbor, connected two long ladders together with ropes to paint the lighthouse towers. *Scituate Historical Society Archives*

81

How do we know so much about life at lighthouse stations long ago? One way is by reading the actual records written by lighthouse keepers. For many years, keepers in the United States were required to keep journals of station activities. The government supplied blank journals, which everyone called logbooks. Many original light station logs survive and provide an important record of the lives of keepers.

Entries in the logbooks were usually short. Keepers were told to record the weather, visitors to the station, including a supply boat, and "any item of interest occurring in the vicinity." Many notations stated basic facts about the weather, such as wind speed or whether it had snowed or rained. In August 1905, a keeper at Cana Island Lighthouse in Wisconsin noted a rare eclipse

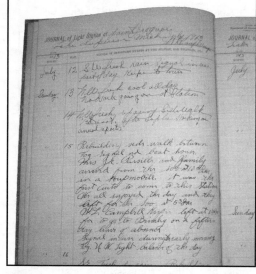

Michigan Lighthouse Conservancy

of the sun at 5:00 A.M. Logs also contained descriptions of the keeper's duties. At Sand Island, Wisconsin, the log for June 1, 1899, included this entry: "Keeper painted bedroom floor and kitchen floor and outhouse floor."

Sometimes, a keeper recorded news of national importance. On September 15, 1901, Charlie Davis of the Copper Harbor range lights in northern Michigan wrote, "I heard the news of the death of President William McKinley yesterday. Was very much shocked and grieved to hear of his untimely death."

It was uncommon for a keeper to express his feelings about his job in a log, but it did happen. On July 4, 1874, the keeper at Pilot Island, Michigan, began his entry with a typical statement about the weather: "Independence Day came in fine after a heavy southeast gale." The ex–Civil War soldier then wrote, "This island affords about as much independence and liberty as Libby Prison [a Civil War prison]." On a positive note, the lighthouse did not have guards, he explained. On the other hand, he concluded, it was easier to communicate with the outside world from prison than from his remote island.

Create a Lighthouse Logbook

Mazie Freeman lived at Maine's Petit Manan Lighthouse as a child when her father was keeper there in the early 20th century. She recalled, "The building I loved most . . . was the log room. It was in this room that I spent many hours reading the old logs, for none had been removed from the station since the lighthouse was built. There were notations about terrible storms, shipwrecks, malfunctions of machinery, and often amusing accounts of landlubbers who had visited the station." You can make a logbook similar to the ones the keepers used.

You'll Need

Old newspapers
2 pieces of heavy cardboard, 8¼ × 11
    inches (21 × 27.9 cm)
Duct tape, about 2 × 10½ inches
    (5.1 × 26.7 cm)
20 sheets of lined notebook paper,
    8 × 10½ inches (20.3 × 26.7 cm)
Glue stick
All-purpose liquid glue
Faux leather or suede, 20 × 11 inches
    (50.8 × 27.9 cm) from fabric store
Two pieces of heavy-weight art paper,
    8¼ × 11 inches (21 × 27.9 cm)

Spread newspapers on your work surface. Place the two pieces of cardboard on top of each other; bind on the left side with duct tape to form the cover. Set aside.

Take one sheet of notebook paper and turn it over. Use the glue stick to put a thin line of glue along the right margin of the paper. Do not extend the glue line more than ½ inch (1.3 cm) in from the side of the paper. Adhere another sheet of paper to the first sheet. Continue to glue all the sheets of notebook paper together this way. When done, turn stack over; let dry.

Place suede fabric face down on work surface. Open cardboard book cover and center on the fabric. You should have about 1½ inches (3.8 cm) of spare fabric on either side. Create a line of all-purpose glue along the left side of the inside front cover about 1¼ inches (3.18 cm) wide. Fold over the suede fabric flap and press into glue to secure. When dry, close the book.

Glue the suede to the outside front and back cardboard covers. Leave excess suede along the duct tape spine so that the book can be opened and closed easily. Next, glue the suede flap to the inside back cover; lay open to dry.

Use the liquid glue to attach one piece of art paper to the inside front cover; lay open to dry. Do the same in the back of the book. Use the liquid glue to attach the pile of notebook pages (facing up) to the inside back cover. Apply pressure for a minute or two to secure; lay open to dry.

Now that your logbook is finished, pretend you are a lighthouse keeper. On the front cover, write "Logbook for _____ Lighthouse" (pick a name), and write the year that you are pretending to live in. After that, begin to fill in the other pages by writing the date down the left column of the left page and adding details across both pages. What is the weather like? Were there any visitors to your station? Special events or holidays? Shipwrecks? Damage to the lighthouse from a storm? You can read parts of real lighthouse logbooks for ideas. Excerpts from logbooks from the following lighthouses are posted online:

Manitou Island, Michigan
www.terrypepper.com/lights/superior/mani
    tou/manitou11.htm

Point Reyes, California
www.nps.gov/pore/history_maritime_
    lhlogs.htm

Another constant task was painting. William O. Simpkins, keeper of Hooper Strait Lighthouse in the Chesapeake Bay in the 1920s, estimated that one-fourth of his time working was spent painting! "Many winter days were spent painting the walls and ceilings in the living quarters," recalled Betty Byrnes. In the spring, the outsides of buildings were painted. Naturally, the most difficult job was painting the lighthouse tower, especially the roof of the lantern room. It is hard to say whether keepers or those on the ground watching found this job more terrifying. "I can remember Dad connecting (by ropes) a sixteen-foot ladder to the top of a thirty-two foot extension ladder," wrote Harold Jennings. Keeper Charles Jennings of Lovells Island in Boston Harbor then hoisted the contraption up the side of the tower. Harold later remarked that it was "a wonder he didn't get killed."

Inspection Time

Have your parents ever inspected your room to see if you cleaned it properly? Imagine having your entire house, garage, and yard inspected at any time—with no warning. Inspections were a regular part of lighthouse living, and a keeper's reputation depended on the results. A few times each year, an inspector arrived to look over the entire light station. The inspections were supposed to be a surprise, but keepers sometimes had advance notice.

Once lighthouses had telephones, keepers would call each other to warn that the inspector was approaching. After boats began flying special flags noting the inspector was aboard, the keeper's family made it a game to see who could notice the boat first. As soon as someone spotted the boat, everyone would do last-minute tidying and change into fancy clothes. The keeper then scurried to put on his dress uniform and cap, which he did not wear for everyday chores. "Inspections were a nuisance, but any person living or employed on government property knows he is subject to inspection at any time," recalled Norma Engel. Children of keepers remember inspectors who donned white gloves to run their fingers over door frames and windowsills looking for dust.

Despite the solemn nature of inspections, they resulted in some funny moments. Betty Byrnes remembered when her mother did not have time to wash all the dishes before an inspection. At the time, people did not have dishwashers in their homes. In an effort to clean up quickly, Mrs. Byrnes tossed all the dishes into a big bread pan, covered them with a cloth, and stuck them in the oven. If the inspector opened the oven door, it would look like bread was baking. He never did.

One day, Glenn Furst's mother put oil on the kitchen floor just before the inspector entered their house at the North Manitou Island Light Station in Michigan. Like floor wax, the oil made the floors shiny and helped protect the wood. This time, though, she used a little too much oil. When the inspector extended his hand to greet Glenn's mother, he slipped on the freshly oiled surface. "He came across that floor waving his arms like a young sea gull attempting its first flight," Glenn later wrote. The inspector caught himself on the handle of a pump used to draw water into the kitchen sink. After he steadied himself, he shook Glenn's mother's hand, and the inspection continued as though nothing had happened.

No Ordinary Job

Many lighthouse keepers were extremely dedicated to their jobs. Some of these men and women had lived around water all their lives. They might have been sailors or relatives of sailors. For this reason, they knew how important it was to keep the lighthouse light shining. "Somehow when we were on the light, we didn't think of it as a job at all," wrote Connie Small, wife of Keeper Elson Small. "It was a calling. We were conscious of the fact that that light was saving a great many lives."

Make a Replica Keeper's Cap

You can make a cap similar to ones worn by keepers when the inspector arrived. The design for this cap is modeled after one detailed in uniform regulations for keepers issued in 1920.

You'll Need

A friend to help you measure

Flexible tape measure

2 pieces of blue craft foam; one 11¾ × 17¾ inches (30 × 45 cm), the other 9 × 12 inches (22.9 × 30.5 cm)*

Scissors

20 brass paper fasteners

Pencil

Heavy cardboard (from pizza box or shipping carton; must be thick enough to insert paper fasteners in its side)

Tacky glue

1 piece of tracing paper or other transparent paper

2 × 4-inch (5.1 × 10.2-cm) piece of black plastic trash bag or clear vinyl tinted black (from a fabric store)

Toothpick

5 inches (12.7 cm) gold fabric trim

4 × 4-inch (10.2 × 10.2-cm) piece of aluminum foil

*If you can't find navy foam, buy any color blue foam, and paint your hat after it is assembled.

Have a friend measure the distance around your head by wrapping the tape measure around it, about 1½ inches (3.8 cm) above your ears. Add 1 inch (2.5 cm) to this number to calculate the band size.

Cut two pieces of 2 × 17¾-inch (5.1 × 45-cm) craft foam. Form a continuous band with the two strips by placing the end of one atop the end of another with an overlap of ½ inch (1.3cm). Connect the strips by sticking two paper fasteners through both pieces of foam; spread out prongs of the fasteners to secure.

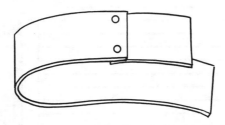

Place the band flat on a table; the heads of the paper fasteners should be facing up. Use scissors and the measuring stick to trim the band size to the desired band length as calculated above. Attach the two ends together to form one continuous foam circle. (The ends should overlap about ½ inch (1.3 cm).

Stand the band up on the cardboard; use tape to affix it to the cardboard. Trace around the inside of the band with your pencil to form the top of the cap, keeping the band as still as possible. (It is better to draw a circle slightly smaller than the band rather than a bigger one.)

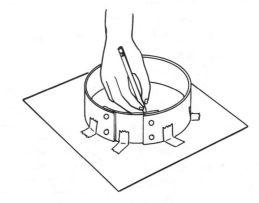

Detach the band from the cardboard and remove tape. Cut the top of your cap out of the cardboard. Place it on the smaller sheet of foam and trace around it. Cut out the foam circle and glue it on the cardboard circle. Trim excess foam or cardboard with scissors so that the edges match.

Stand the band on the table. Use two hands to press the foam/cardboard circle, with the foam side down, through the band onto the table. Don't worry if it's a tight squeeze; the foam is somewhat flexible.

(If it does not fit, trim the foam/cardboard circle slightly and try again.) The fasteners used to make the band should be in the back of the cap, so position the foam/cardboard circle accordingly. To attach the foam/cardboard top to the band, insert paper fasteners, about 1 inch (2.5 cm) apart, through the band and into the cardboard.

Trace the visor pattern, then cut a visor out of foam. Crease the visor as indicated on the pattern, applying pressure for several seconds to create a visible crease. (It will not stay folded, but the crease will help later.) Apply tacky glue as indicated on pattern. Carefully press the visor onto the inside of the band, folding along the crease to help the visor stay in position. Hold until secure; let dry.

For finishing touches, cut out a small piece of black plastic or vinyl, in the shape shown on pattern. Glue to the top of the visor to give it the appearance of a sun visor. Cut a simple lighthouse from aluminum foil and place on the front of the cap band. Use toothpick to apply glue to trim; attach trim to cap.

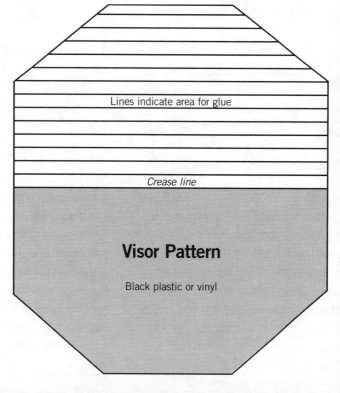

Lines indicate area for glue

Crease line

Visor Pattern

Black plastic or vinyl

Elizabeth Whitney Williams came to realize the same thing, even during one of the worst times of her life. Williams assisted her sickly husband at Harbor Point Lighthouse on Michigan's Beaver Island. In 1872, her husband died while trying to rescue a man from a leaking schooner. As she grieved, Williams felt weak. Yet she soon realized that others needed her to keep the light shining. "Nothing could rouse me but that thought, then all my life and energy was given to the work which now seemed was given me to do," she later wrote. After a few weeks, she received an official appointment as keeper.

Keepers' children also understood that there was no holiday for the hardworking lighthouse keeper. "No matter what we were doing, the maintenance of the light and the fog signal came first," Philmore Wass recalled. "Just because it was Christmas did not mean that a ship might not be depending upon these guides to stay on her course and away from the rocks and reefs."

LIFE ABOARD A FLOATING LIGHTHOUSE

The morning of May 15, 1934, was a foggy one 40 miles (64 km) off the coast of Nantucket Island in Massachusetts. The 11 men who worked on Lightship No. 117, the *Nantucket*, were used to the thick mist. No matter what the weather, their boat was anchored in the same spot to warn sailors of dangerous shoals. On this morning, the ship's foghorn boomed its warning.

Not far away, the British luxury liner *Olympic* moved through the dense fog toward the lightship. The sailors aboard the *Olympic*, the sister ship of the *Titanic*, knew about the lightship and planned to change their course before reaching it. Instead, they made a terrible mistake. Suddenly at 10:06 A.M., their 47,000-ton-ship (over 42,000 metric tons) sliced the lightship in two, sinking it in the deep, cold water of the Atlantic Ocean. Four crew members of the *Nantucket* went down with their ship. The crew of the *Olympic* quickly launched lifeboats in an effort to save

Buffalo Light Vessel No. 98, as depicted in *The United States Lighthouse Service 1915*, published by the federal government. *University of Iowa Libraries*

the others. Seven others were plucked from the sea, but three died later.

Life aboard a floating lighthouse, or lightship, could be dangerous and unpredictable. In fact, boats had serious collisions with lightships about 150 times in U.S. history. Lightships also experienced many other bumps and scrapes. During World War I, the crew aboard the *Diamond Shoals* lightship in North Carolina sent out an electronic signal to let boaters know that an enemy submarine was nearby. After the crew safely escaped the lightship in small boats, the German sub fired on the lightship, sinking it.

High winds and strong storms often threatened lightships, which were moored in

places where it was impossible to build a lighthouse. In November 1913, a gale on Lake Erie caused the *Buffalo* lightship to go down. All the boat's crew members died. A few days after the disaster, a board from the ship washed ashore. The captain had written a last-minute message to his wife. It read, "Goodbye, Nellie, ship is breaking up fast—Williams."

In spite of these dangers, life on a lightship was boring most of the time. The men stationed aboard lightships did the same job day after day. Their families were not allowed to live with them. Unlike keepers at many lighthouses, they could not go to town or invite visitors over for dinner. A captain of one lightship explained his situation this way: "If it weren't for the disgrace it would bring on my family I'd rather go to State's prison." A writer at the time said that life on a lightship seemed like "a term of solitary confinement combined with the horrors of seasickness." For many years in the 1800s, men aboard the *Nantucket* passed the time by weaving wooden baskets. The baskets of various sizes nested, or sat inside, one another. Even today, these types of baskets are known as Nantucket Lightship baskets.

Chapter Seven

Lighthouses Today

California's Cabrillo National Monument offers a panoramic view of San Diego and its harbor. From one angle, visitors can see the many modern skyscrapers that make up the city's skyline. In the water below, a submarine or navy warship might be steaming in or out of the harbor. In the sky above are exhaust trails left by modern jets. In the midst of the grounds of the national monument, though, stands a reminder of another time: the Old Point Loma Lighthouse. First lighted in 1855, the lighthouse looks a bit like a tidy, ordinary house, except for the short brick tower rising out of its roof.

The condition of the Old Point Loma Lighthouse, as shown in this old postcard (left), deteriorated quickly after the light was discontinued and the keeper's family moved out. *Author's Collection*

The restored Old Point Loma Lighthouse today (top). *Cabrillo National Monument*

When you step into the small home, you step into another era. Inside the kitchen is an old-fashioned stove powered not by natural gas or electricity but by wood. Electric lamps resembling oil lamps provide the only light besides sunlight. Upstairs in one bedroom, the keeper's blue dress uniform is laid out carefully on a bed. In the children's bedroom, which is divided by a dressing screen, a guitar sits on one bed, as if a keeper's child just left to do chores or play outside. Lucky visitors may encounter a man portraying Robert Israel, the last keeper of the Old Point Loma Lighthouse, who describes the work of a keeper. The real Keeper Israel served at the Old Point Loma Lighthouse from 1871 until 1891.

The Old Point Loma Lighthouse has not always looked this way. In 1891, the Israels moved down the hill to the New Point Loma Lighthouse. The old lighthouse had been built so high that fog often blocked its light, so the government built another tower closer to the water. When the old lighthouse was abandoned, its condition deteriorated quickly, and the lighthouse quickly became an eyesore.

The Old Point Loma Lighthouse is one of many lighthouses that have been restored inside and out. How do we know what a lighthouse looked like long ago? People working to restore old buildings must do a lot of detective work. Instead of analyzing DNA evidence as police do, they study old documents and photos to learn as much as possible about life during another era. When it is impossible to uncover details about a particular lighthouse, people use what they know about other lighthouses operating at the same time to restore a building.

Government records provide a lot of information, too. Architectural drawings give a snapshot of what the lighthouse and keeper's house looked like when they were new. Annual lists produced by the government for boaters describe daymarks, or how the outsides of lighthouses were painted. Other records show when supplies were delivered to the station. This way, people learned that Old Point Loma got a new cooking stove and pipe in 1861.

The furniture, clothing, and other things in the Old Point Loma Lighthouse have been picked to give visitors a good idea what the keeper's home really looked like. *Cabrillo National Monument*

Information recorded by the keepers is invaluable. From logbooks kept by keepers, it is possible to learn details, such as the type of fence at a station or what color the keeper's house was painted inside. Letters written by the keeper to an inspector might describe a problem or explain how a storm damaged the property. Keeper Israel once wrote a letter telling how his assistant had whitewashed the fence and stable. He complained, though, that the man did not have a horse for the corral, nor was he interested in the garden or chickens. These details let people working to restore the lighthouse know what the entire property looked like, not just the keeper's house.

Saving Lighthouses

At Point Loma and other places across the country, renovating an old lighthouse and turning it into a museum takes a lot of time and money. That's because buildings at light stations were neglected when lighthouses were discontinued or automated. At the time, few people realized that someone should take care of the buildings. As long as an automated light worked, the Coast Guard was doing its job to protect boaters.

After lighthouses were automated or discontinued, their condition went downhill quickly. Over time, metal rusted, paint chipped, and plaster wore off. Animals and birds caused damage, too. Termites gnawed away at wood, and mice and wasps built nests that were hard to remove. Gulls and pigeons splattered buildings with guano, also known as poop. Vandals defaced unoccupied buildings; some lighthouses were destroyed by fire.

Sometimes the Coast Guard contributed to the decay when their keepers left. Pipes were pulled out, flooding buildings. Pipes that remained often burst in cold weather.

Either way, moisture inside a lighthouse rotted wood and helped mold grow. Bathroom fixtures and electrical wiring were ripped out, too. Some historic items were tossed in the water or thrown away. Even historic lantern rooms were changed or removed to make way for automatic lights. In some cases, lighthouses were simply torn down to make way for another building.

Gradually, people began to realize that it was worth saving lighthouses. Why? Some people fondly remember visiting a lighthouse as children; seeing the lighthouse

The Shinnecook, New York, Lighthouse as it is being torn down. *U.S. Coast Guard Historian's Office*

Write a Lighthouse Poem

Rachel Field (1894–1942) was a famous author in the first part of the 20th century. She won the Newbery Medal for children's literature in 1929. At one point in her life, Ms. Field spent her summers on Sutton Island off the coast of Maine, and she often wrote poems about island life, boats, lighthouses, and the nature she noticed around her. You can use one of her poems as inspiration to write your own lighthouse poem.

You'll Need

A few sheets of lined notebook paper or
    writing journal
Pencil or pen

Read Rachel Field's poem, "I'd Like to Be a Lighthouse," right.

I'd like to be a lighthouse

All scrubbed and painted white.

I'd like to be a lighthouse

And stay awake all night

To keep my eye on everything

That sails my patch of sea;

I'd like to be a lighthouse

With the ships all watching me.

Think about what it would be like to be a lighthouse. Structure your own poem of eight lines or more using the phrase, "I'd like to be a lighthouse" for some of the lines. Think about which lines should rhyme. When you are done, draw a picture to illustrate your poem.

---

try. Restored lighthouses have another benefit: they can draw visitors to an area, which helps local businesses succeed.

As people have worked to save old lighthouses, they have found many uses for them. Many display exhibits about life at a lighthouse and invite visitors to learn about local history. Some are private homes, and several have been converted into inns where people can spend the night while on vacation. Lighthouses owned by towns or parks serve as housing or offices. A few lighthouses serve as research stations for people studying wildlife in remote areas. Tillamook Rock Lighthouse in Oregon has a unique purpose. It is now a columbarium, or place where the ashes of dead people are kept. Even when lighthouses are not open to the public, many have been fixed up on the outside and attract visitors to an area.

Human factors like neglect and vandalism certainly have been responsible for decay and destruction of lighthouses. But there is also a serious natural threat to many lighthouses: erosion. By necessity, lighthouses were built near the water's edge, where wind and waves can wear away at the shoreline. The process of erosion may undermine a lighthouse foundation or the cliff it is standing on. Special fences, plants, even large piles of rocks, have been used to slow the process. When nothing else works, the last resort is to move the lighthouse. In the

brings back pleasant memories. Boaters like knowing that a lighthouse stands watch, just in case their high-tech systems fail. Still others appreciate the history lessons old buildings can teach us. Learning about oil lamps and glass lenses may get people thinking about how technology constantly changes. Knowing about lighthouses gives us a sense of our nation's past, of a time when the sea was vital to the growth of the coun-

At Burnt Island Lighthouse in Maine, ex-Keeper James Buotte and others portray Keeper Joseph Muise and his family as they would have appeared when they tended the lighthouse in 1950. *Maine Department of Marine Resources*

(2,540 metric tons). One hundred hydraulic jacks helped lift it. After the tower was lifted onto a support framework, additional hydraulic jacks helped propel the structure along rollers, similar to railroad tracks. It took more than three weeks to move the lighthouse back from the ocean. The lighthouse traveled so slowly that people who came to watch could barely detect any motion.

1980s and 1990s, five lighthouses in New England were moved back from the edges of cliffs. No lighthouse moving project got as much attention as one in 1999, however.

That summer, North Carolina's Cape Hatteras Lighthouse was moved about 2,500 feet (762 m) inland. People involved in the project liked to call it "The Move of the Century." That seems to be an apt description. After all, the black-and-white striped lighthouse is the tallest in the United States, and it weighs a whopping 2,800 tons

A New Generation of Keepers

When you were younger, you may have read *The Little Red Lighthouse and the Great Gray Bridge*. Generations of children have fallen in love with this picture book, which was first published in 1942. The book tells the story of a small lighthouse trying to figure out its role after a bridge with bright lights is built nearby. Many people are surprised to

The Cape Hatteras Lighthouse moves toward its new destination away from the ocean. *Mike Booher for the National Park Service*

Witness the Power of Hydraulics

The technology used for lifting heavy buildings is around us every-day. Hydraulic jacks like those used to move the Cape Hatteras Lighthouse are used to support partially collapsed buildings after earthquakes and to raise vehicles at repair shops. Hydraulic systems also help cars brake and dump trucks dump their loads. The systems work because water and other fluids cannot be compressed. Although most hydraulic systems today use oil, you can use water to see how hydraulics work.

You'll Need

A friend

1 10-ml oral medication syringe (standard size available at pharmacies)

1 oral medication syringe larger than 10 ml; 35-ml works well (ask for a large syringe at a pet store, veterinary office, or farm supply store)

18-inch (45.8-cm) piece of plastic tubing to connect the two (¼-inch outside diameter tubing will probably work, but take syringes along when buying tubing to be sure.)

Duct tape

Bowl filled with water colored with food coloring, sitting in a sink

Ruler

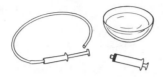

Remove the plunger from the 10-ml syringe. At the other end of the syringe, push the tubing along the tip as far as possible; secure with tape. Twist the tape tightly around the tubing to prevent leaks. Insert the 35-ml syringe into the bowl of colored water, and draw the plunger up slowly until the syringe is full.

Attach the free end of tubing to the tip of the 35-ml syringe; secure with tape, as above. Have your friend hold the 10-ml syringe over the bowl, while you press the plunger of the 35-ml syringe in until the 10-ml syringe is full. Replace the plunger of the 10-ml syringe, forcing the water back into the 35-ml syringe. There should not be any visible air bubbles in either

syringe or the tubing now. You are now ready to start your demonstration.

Push the plunger of the 35-mil syringe in slightly; notice how far the plunger of the 10-mil syringe rises. Empty the water back into the 35-mil syringe by pressing down on the plunger of the 10-mil syringe. Again, note the upward movement of the plunger of the larger syringe. Now repeat the demonstration, this time using the ruler to measure exactly how far each plunger moves when all the water goes from syringe to syringe. Is one plunger easier to push than the other? Why do you think this is? When a hydraulic jack is used to move a lighthouse, do you think the fluid flows from a big area to a small one or vice versa?

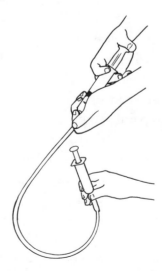

learn that the book was based on a real lighthouse. The red, cast-iron tower still stands in a park in New York City. Although its real name is the Jeffrey's Hook Lighthouse, most people call it "Little Red."

Author Hildegarde Swift lived in New York City near "Little Red," and it inspired her story. Swift watched as a massive bridge was built to link New York City and New Jersey. When the George Washington Bridge, as it is now called, opened in 1931, people were glad they did not have to take a ferry across the river anymore. Lights on the bridge shined brightly enough to make the lighthouse obsolete. As a result, the Coast Guard stopped using the lighthouse in 1947 and put it up for sale in 1951.

No one was prepared for what happened next. When young New Yorkers found out about the sale, they were very upset. They had fallen in love with "Little Red" because of Swift's book. Kids collected pennies, nickels, and dimes in the hopes they could save the lighthouse. Instead of selling it, the federal government turned the structure over to the city. Through the years, children continued to play a role in taking care of "Little Red." One year, a preschool class helped cover it with a new coat of red paint. When the lighthouse was in bad condition in the 1980s, the child of a government official stepped in. He convinced his father that the city should find the money to preserve the lighthouse.

New York's Little Red Lighthouse is dwarfed by the nearby George Washington Bridge in this undated photo. *U.S. Coast Guard Historian's Office*

The St. Helena, Michigan, Light Station before and after restoration. *Great Lakes Lighthouse Keepers Association*

Today, the Little Red Lighthouse stands as a shining example of what children can do to make a difference in their towns and cities. "Little Red" may have been the first lighthouse that children helped out, but it would not be the last. In 1965, the Charlotte-Genesee Lighthouse in Rochester, New York, was scheduled to be torn down. High school students got people to sign petitions in favor of keeping the lighthouse. The structure was saved, and it was turned over to a historical society.

More recently, students on Michigan's Beaver Island got involved in helping out a local lighthouse. The fifth and sixth graders

A GHOST OF A CHANCE: STRANGE LIGHTHOUSE HAPPENINGS

Have you ever seen a ghost? Plenty of people who visit lighthouses believe they have. The Point Lookout Lighthouse in Maryland is said to be haunted by several ghosts. Doors open and shut for no apparent reason. Ghosts talk. One female ghost dressed in a long blue skirt and white shirt is believed to be Ann Davis, an early keeper. The ghost of Joseph Haney also roams the grounds, according to some witnesses. He died in a shipwreck not far from the lighthouse in 1878. The fact that Civil War prisoners died nearby only adds to the eerie atmosphere at Point Lookout. Other lighthouses said to be haunted include Minot's Ledge, Massachusetts; Seguin Lighthouse, Maine; St. Simons Lighthouse, Georgia; and Yaquina Bay Lighthouse, Oregon.

learned how to calculate the number of bricks in the St. James Lighthouse. They also estimated how many bricks would need to be replaced to preserve the tower. Michigan high school students constructed a model of the Grand Island East Channel Lighthouse. The realistic-looking model was put on display to educate people about the need to preserve the lighthouse. At a middle school in New Hampshire, a group calling itself "The Lighthouse Kids" raised money to restore the decaying White Island Lighthouse.

On a remote island in Michigan, students have done more than raise money and awareness about a lighthouse. They have actually done the physical labor of fixing up the buildings at the St. Helena Light Station. The light station was in shambles more than 20 years ago. Shingles were missing from the roof of the keeper's house. Fires set by vandals had damaged the second floor. Plaster covered the floors, and a pair of ospreys lived in the lantern room of the lighthouse tower. Boy Scouts and other youth groups have spent time there scraping paint, hammering boards, and repainting structures. They have hauled trash away, rebuilt a boathouse, and restored an outhouse. Along with people everywhere who work to save lighthouses, these students are the "Keepers of Tomorrow."

 # THAT'S A LiGHTHOUSE?!

The white-and-red-striped tower near Sabine Pass, Louisiana, looks more like a spaceship than a lighthouse. But this brick structure was built long before people traveled in space, so its designer had no way of knowing what a rocket ship would look like. Daniel Leadbetter, an Army engineer, simply wanted a way to build a sturdy structure in the sandy soil. The octagonal lighthouse has six concrete braces, or buttresses, that flare out near the bottom of the tower to steady it. His unusual design succeeded. The lighthouse has stood along the border of Louisiana and Texas since 1856. Today, it is in fragile condition.

What do you see when you look at this photo of a Buffalo, New York, building? It's a bottle, it's an upside down wine glass, it's . . . a lighthouse. Its official name is the Buffalo North Breakwater South End Light, but people just call it "the bottle light." Built in 1903 from cast iron, the short white tower has small round windows that look like ship portholes. It was moved from its original location and now stands at water's edge on a Coast Guard base that will become a park.

Another one just like it stands in a park where the Dunkirk, New York, lighthouse is located. It too was moved from it's original location at the Buffalo Harbor's south entrance.

The Sabine Pass Lighthouse. *The U.S. Coast Guard Historian's Office*

The Buffalo North Breakwater South End Light. *Michael N. Vogel*

98

 **Resources**

Web Sites to Explore

There is a vast amount of lighthouse information on the Internet. These comprehensive sites are useful for exploring lighthouse history and for finding your way to lighthouses you might want to visit.

Lighthouse Digest magazine
www.lighthousedigest.com

Read current and back issues of this magazine for lighthouse enthusiasts; check out the "Doomsday List" of endangered lighthouses. Articles cover a wide variety of topics, such as keepers' lives, lighthouse history, and restoration projects; many are accompanied by historic photos.

The Lighthouse Directory
www.unc.edu/~rowlett/lighthouse/

If you are looking for information about lighthouses in other countries, check out this site. Maintained by a mathematics professor with a passion for lighthouses, it compiles photos and brief histories of hundreds of lighthouses around the world. Site also includes up-to-date news about lighthouses.

Lighthouse Explorer Database (by Lighthouse Depot)
www.lighthousedepot.com/database/searchdatabase.cfm

Database includes brief information about 7,000+ lighthouses around the world. Search by U.S. state, Canadian province, country, or lighthouse name. Includes names of keepers at many U.S. light stations and brief descriptions of light characteristics.

Lighthousefriends.com
www.lighthousefriends.com

This site offers wonderful maps showing locations of all lighthouses in a particular state. Click on a lighthouse name from each state map to obtain photos, histories, and driving directions. Some histories are detailed and include bibliographies.

The Lighthouse People
www.thelighthousepeople.com

A husband-and-wife team, known as "the Lighthouse People," have posted hundreds of photos of U.S. lighthouses on this site, as well as stories of their adventures traveling to remote lighthouses.

National Park Service's Inventory of Historic Light Stations
www.cr.nps.gov/maritime/ltsum.htm

Organized by state, this site lists historic lighthouses, the year in which they were built, and their current use.

National Park Service's List of Publicly Accessible Lighthouses
www.cr.nps.gov/maritime/ltaccess.html

Arranged by region, this site lets you know whether you can visit the grounds of a lighthouse, see a lighthouse museum, or climb the tower; includes addresses and brief directions.

National Park Service's Report on Lightships in the United States
www.cr.nps.gov/maritime/ltshipnhl theme.htm

Provides a detailed history of the construction and evolution of lightships in the United States.

National Park Service's Maritime Heritage Program
www.cr.nps.gov/maritime

Click on "Lighthouse Heritage" on this top-notch site to read explanations of lighthouse types, review detailed histories of lighthouses nominated for National Historic Landmark Status, and to view photos of Fresnel lenses at different lighthouses. Also includes information on the National Historic Lighthouse Preservation Act of 2000.

New England Lighthouses: A Virtual Guide
http://lighthouse.cc

Maintained by author Jeremy D'Entremont, this thorough site includes a detailed history of New England's lighthouses, as well as current and hard-to-find historic photos. It lists lighthouses by state and provides information on New England lighthouse tours and special events. A bibliography of sources for each lighthouse is included. Site also includes a long list of lighthouses around the world where you can spend the night.

Public Broadcasting Service's Legendary Lighthouses
www.pbs.org/legendarylighthouses

Designed to supplement PBS' *Legendary Lighthouses* series, this site includes photos and histories of lighthouses featured on the shows and information about their keepers and the people restoring them.

Seeing the Light: Lighthouses of the Western Great Lakes
www.terrypepper.com/lights

This comprehensive site contains photos, histories (with a bibliography for each lighthouse), and directions to each lighthouse, arranged by the lake on which they appear. Database section lists lighthouses by architectural type, type of lens, and other characteristics. Beyond that, there is much historical information about

lighting technology, fog signals, and lighthouses in general.

U.S. Coast Guard Historian's Office
www.uscg.mil/hq/g-cp/history/collect.html

A great resource for learning more about lighthouses and lightships. Includes a detailed time line, fun facts, information on lighthouse types, photos of light keepers, and an expanded version of the National Park Service's Inventory of Historic Lighthouse Stations with photos.

U.S. Coast Guard Light List
www.navcen.uscg.gov

Click on "Light List and Corrections" from the menu on the home page to review a list of all lighted aids to navigation, including lighthouses. Details to aid sailors include the geographic position of each lighthouse, a description of the light characteristic, and information about the structure's appearance.

U.S. Coast Guard Index of Lightship Station Assignments
www.uscg.mil/hq/g-cp/history/Lightship_Station_Index.html

Offers brief historical sketches of more than 100 lightship stations, including a list of the different vessels that served those stations.

Organizations

Here are some of the major groups for people interested in learning more about lighthouses and/or restoring them. In addition to the groups listed here, there are dozens more devoted to saving and/or promoting a single lighthouse.

American Lighthouse Foundation
www.lighthousefoundation.org

ALF is dedicated to the preservation and restoration of lighthouses, lightships, and lifesaving stations in the United States; the home page has links to chapters devoted to specific lighthouses.

Association of Lighthouse Keepers
www.alk.org.uk

Founded by active and retired lighthouse keepers, membership in this British organization is open to lighthouse enthusiasts around the world. Site includes photos and histories of lighthouses throughout Great Britain.

Florida Lighthouse Association
www.floridalighthouses.org

The association's Web site includes photos, background information, and visitor information about the state's lighthouses.

Friends of Flying Santa
www.flyingsanta.org

This group is dedicated to making sure the Flying Santa tradition continues today in the Northeast. Its site includes extensive historical information and photos about the history of the Flying Santa, who delivers toys and goodies to lighthouse and Coast Guard families at Christmas.

Great Lakes Lighthouse Keepers Association
www.gllka.com

Dedicated to lighthouses along the Great Lakes, this organization has been successful in getting young people involved in restoration efforts. The group's Web site includes photos and details on the St. Helena, Michigan, restoration project.

Hudson River Lighthouse Coalition
www.hudsonlights.com

Visitor information and histories of seven lighthouses along New York's Hudson River.

International Association of Marine Aids to Navigation and Lighthouse Authorities
www.iala-aism.org/web/index.html

This organization is devoted to authorities around the world that oversee lighthouses.

Lighthouse Stamp Society
www.lighthousestampsociety.org

Hundreds of photos of lighthouse stamps from around the world can be found here.

Michigan Lighthouse Conservancy
www.michiganlights.com

Although this group is dedicated to lighthouses in Michigan (and there are plenty of them), it has valuable resources for anyone wanting to learn more about lighthouses in general. Of special note is a section on lighthouse keepers' tools with color photos.

New Jersey Lighthouse Society
www.njlhs.org

The NJLHS has an exceptional Web site loaded with historical information, old photos, and transcribed documents about the history of the state's lighthouses. Includes time line of New Jersey lighthouse history.

The Outer Banks Lighthouse Society
www.outer-banks.com/lighthouse-society

If you live in North Carolina or plan to go there, follow the tour of the state's lighthouses on this Web site for information important to visitors.

United States Lighthouse Society
www.uslhs.org

Publisher of *The Keeper's Log*, an excellent magazine of lighthouse history, the USLHS also offers lighthouse trivia on its Web site and information about lighthouses where you can spend the night. The group's site includes links to regional chapters, such as the Chesapeake Bay and Long Island chapters, as well as those focusing on a single lighthouse.

Washington Lightkeepers Association
www.walightkeepers.com

This group is dedicated to the preservation and restoration of lighthouses and lightships in Washington state.

World Lighthouse Society
www.worldlighthouses.org

This international group is devoted to saving lighthouses and light vessels around the world.

Places to Visit

Museums

Coast Guard Museum
U.S. Coast Guard Academy
New London, Connecticut
(860) 444-8511
www.uscg.mil/hq/g-cp/museum/
museumindex.asp

Dedicated to all facets of Coast Guard history, this museum includes a first order Fresnel lens from Thacher Island, Massachusetts.

Coast Guard Museum Northwest
Seattle, Washington
(206) 217-6993
www.rexmwess.com/cgpatchs/cogard
museum.html

See lighthouse and buoy lenses, Coast Guard uniforms, a Lighthouse Service clock, and other items related to the history of the Coast Guard in the Pacific Northwest.

Maine Lighthouse Museum
(formerly Shore Village Museum)
Rockland, Maine
(207) 594-3301
www.mainelighthousemuseum.com

This museum contains the largest collection of lighthouse lenses in the United States, including many old Fresnel lenses, as well as many other artifacts.

Historic Lighthouses You Can Climb

If you would like to visit a historic lighthouse once (or still) operated by the government and climb the tower, consult this list. Lighthouses listed are open several times a year; many are open only in the summer or on summer weekends. Some lighthouses

have a minimum age or height requirement to climb the tower. In most cases, if you are old enough to read this book, you should be able to climb the tower.

See the museum listing on page 111 for lighthouses that are closed to the public but offer access to the base of the tower and/or a nearby museum or exhibits. Hundreds more lighthouses in parks and on islands and piers are not included. In many cases, you can walk around the exterior of those structures and take pictures but cannot get inside. Before visiting, it's a good idea to call ahead to check hours, tour times, etc.

CALIFORNIA

Battery Point Lighthouse
Crescent City
(707) 464-3089
www.delnortehistory.org/lighthouse

East Brother Light Station
East Brother Island
(510) 233-2385
www.ebls.org

Old Point Loma Lighthouse / Cabrillo
National Monument
San Diego
(619) 557-5450
www.nps.gov/cabr

Point Arena Lighthouse and Museum
Point Arena
(707) 882-2777
www.pointarenalighthouse.com

Point Fermin Lighthouse
San Pedro
(310) 241-0684
www.pointferminlighthouse.org

Point San Luis Lighthouse
Avila Beach
(805) 546-4904
www.sanluislighthouse.org

Point Sur Lighthouse / Point Sur State
Historic Park
Big Sur
(831) 625-4419
www.pointsur.org

Point Vicente Lighthouse
Rancho Palos Verdes
(310) 541-0334
www.palosverdes.com/pvlight

St. George Reef Lighthouse
St. George Reef (near Crescent City)
(707) 464-8299
www.stgeorgereeflighthouse.us
Note: Because access is by helicopter only, the cost of visiting is prohibative for many people.

CONNECTICUT

Five Mile Point Lighthouse (New Haven
Harbor Light) / Lighthouse Point Park
New Haven
(203) 946-8790
www.cityofnewhaven.com/Parks/ranger/
eastshore.asp#Tours%20of%20the%20Lighth
ouse

New London Ledge Lighthouse
New London
(860) 445-9007
www.oceanology.org/lighthouse.html

Sheffield Island Lighthouse
Norwalk
(203) 838-9444
www.seaport.org/sheffield_island.htm

Stonington Harbor Lighthouse / Old
Lighthouse Museum
Stonington
(860) 535-1440
www.stoningtonhistory.org/light.htm

DELAWARE

Delaware Breakwater East End Lighthouse
Lewes
www.delawarebaylights.org

Harbor of Refuge Lighthouse
Lewes
www.delawarebaylights.org

FLORIDA

Cape Florida Lighthouse / Bill Baggs Cape
Florida State Park
Key Biscayne
(305) 361-5811
www.floridastateparks.org/capeflorida

Jupiter Inlet Lighthouse
Jupiter Inlet
(561) 747-6639
www.lrhs.org/JIL.htm

Key West Lighthouse and Keeper's Quarters
Museum
Key West
(305) 294-0012
www.kwahs.com/lighthouse.htm

Ponce de Leon Inlet Light Station
Ponce Inlet
(386) 761-1821
www.ponceinlet.org

St. Augustine Lighthouse and Museum
St. Augustine
(904) 829-0745
www.staugustinelighthouse.com

GEORGIA

St. Simons Island Lighthouse Museum
St. Simons Island
(912) 638-4666
www.saintsimonslighthouse.org

Sapelo Island Light / Sapelo Island Reserve
Sapelo Island
(912) 437-3224
www.gastateparks.org/info/sapelo

Tybee Island Light Station
Tybee Island
(912) 786-5801
www.tybeelighthouse.org

ILLINOIS

Grosse Point Lighthouse
Evanston
(847) 328-6961
www.grossepointlighthouse.net

INDIANA

Michigan City Lighthouse / Old Lighthouse
Museum
Michigan City
(219) 872-6133
www.michigancity.com/MCHistorical/
index.html

MAINE

Burnt Island Lighthouse
Burnt Island
(207) 633-9559
www.maine.gov/dmr/education/burntisle.htm

Pemaquid Point Lighthouse
Bristol
(207) 563-2739
www.lighthousefoundation.org/alf_lights/
pemaquidpoint/pemaquid_info.htm

Rockland Breakwater Lighthouse
Rockland
(207) 785-4609
www.rocklandlighthouse.com

Seguin Island Light Station
Seguin Island
(207) 443-4808
www.seguinisland.org

Spring Point Ledge Lighthouse
South Portland
(207) 699-2676
(207) 799-6337
www.springpointlight.org
www.portlandharbormuseum.org

MARYLAND

Concord Point Lighthouse
Havre de Grace
(410) 939-3213
www.nps.gov/history/maritime/light/
concord.htm

Drum Point Lighthouse / Calvert Marine
Museum
Solomons
(410) 326-2042
www.calvertmarinemuseum.com

Hooper Strait Lighthouse / Chesapeake Bay
Maritime Museum
St. Michael's
(410) 745-2916
www.cbmm.org/wh_exhib_lhouse.html

Piney Point Lighthouse, Museum, and
Historic Park
Callaway
(301) 769-2222
(301) 994-1471
www.co.saint-marys.md.us/recreate/museums/
ppl.asp

Point Lookout Lighthouse / Point Lookout
State Park
Scotland
(301) 872-5688
www.pllps.org/index.html
www.dnr.state.md.us/publiclands/southern/
pointlookout.html

Seven Foot Knoll Lighthouse / Baltimore
Maritime Museum
Baltimore
(410) 396-3453
www.baltomaritimemuseum.org/museums_
lighthouse.php

Thomas Point Shoal Lighthouse
Annapolis
(800) 690-5080
www.thomaspointlighthouse.org

Turkey Point Light Station / Elk Neck
State Park
North East
(410) 287-8170
(410) 287-5333
www.tpls.org
www.dnr.state.md.us/publiclands/central/
elkneck.html

MASSACHUSETTS

Bass River Lighthouse / The Lighthouse Inn
West Dennis
(508) 398-2244
www.lighthouseinn.com

Boston Lighthouse / Boston Harbor Islands
National Recreation Area
Little Brewster Island
(617) 223-8666
www.nps.gov/boha

Cape Ann Light Station on Thacher Island
(only one of two towers is open to public)
Thacher Island
(978) 546-7697
www.thacherisland.org

Cape Cod Highland Lighthouse / Cape Cod
National Seashore
North Truro
(508) 487-1121
http://trurohistorical.org
www.nps.gov/caco

Cape Poge Lighthouse / Cape Poge Wildlife
Refuge
Martha's Vineyard
(508) 627-3599
www.thetrustees.org/capepogewildliferefuge.cfm

Chatham Lighthouse
Chatham
www.uscg.mil/d1/Units/gruwh/
stachatham/chatham_lighthouse.htm

East Chop Lighthouse
Martha's Vineyard
(508) 627-4441
www.marthasvineyardhistory.org

Gay Head Lighthouse
Martha's Vineyard
(508) 627-4441
www.marthasvineyardhistory.org

Nauset Lighthouse / Cape Cod National
Seashore
Eastham
(508) 240-2612
www.nausetlight.org
www.nps.gov/caco

Ned's Point Lighthouse
Mattapoisett
E-mail: nedspointlight@comcast.net

Nobska Point Lighthouse
Woods Hole
(508) 548-8500
www.lighthouse.cc/hobska/

Plum Island Lighthouse (Newburyport
Harbor Light)
Newburyport
(978) 462-4770
www.newburyportharborlighthouseplumis.org

Race Point Lighthouse
Provincetown
(508) 487-9930
www.racepointlighthouse.net

Scituate Lighthouse
Scituate
(781) 545-1083
www.scituatehistoricalsociety.org/
sites_lighthouse.html

Three Sisters of Nauset / Cape Cod National
Seashore (one tower is open during tours)
Eastham
(508) 255-3421
www.nps.gov/caco

MICHIGAN

Au Sable Light Station / Pictured Rocks
National Lakeshore
Grand Marais
(906) 387-3700
www.nps.gov/piro

Beaver Island Light Station
Beaver Island
www.beaverislandlighthouse.org

Big Sable Point Lighthouse / Ludington
State Park
Ludington
(231) 845-7343
www.bigsablelighthouse.org
www.michigandnr.com/parksandtrails/Parks
andTrailsInfo.aspx?id=468

Cheboygan River Front Range Light
Cheboygan
(231) 436-5580 (Great Lakes Lighthouse
Keepers Association)

DeTour Reef Light
DeTour Reef (near Drummond Island)
(906) 493-6609
www.drlps.com

Eagle Harbor Lighthouse
Eagle Harbor
(906) 289-4990
www.keweenawhistory.org/eh.html

Fort Gratiot Lighthouse / Port Huron
Museum
Port Huron
(810) 982-0891
www.phmuseum.org/lighthouse.html

Grand Traverse Lighthouse Museum /
Leelanau State Park
Northport
(231) 386-7195
(231) 386-5422
www.grandtraverselighthouse.com
www.michigandnr.com/parksandtrails/Parks
andTrailsInfo.aspx?id=467

Jacobsville Lighthouse Inn Bed and
Breakfast
Jacobsville
(906) 523-4137
www.jacobsvillelighthouse.com

Little Sable Point Lighthouse / Silver Lake
State Park
Mears
(231) 873-3083
www.michigan.gov/dnr/0,1607,7-153-
10365_15070-34760—,00.html

Ludington North Breakwater Light
Ludington
(231) 845-7343
www.nps.gov/history/maritime/light/lud-
ingbk.htm

New Presque Isle Lighthouse
Presque Isle
(989) 595-9917
www.alpenacvb.com/
new-and-old-presque-isle-lighthouses-40/

Old Mackinac Point Lighthouse
Mackinaw City
(231) 436-4100
www.mackinacparks.com/parks/old-mac
inac-point-lighthouse_11

Old Presque Isle Lighthouse
Presque Isle
(989) 595-6979
www.alpenacvb.com/
new-and-old-presque-isle-lighthouses-40/

Ontonagon Lighthouse
Ontonagon
(906) 884-6165
www.ontonagonmuseum.org/lighthouse1.htm

Peninsula Point Lighthouse / Hiawatha
National Forest
Rapid River
(906) 474-6442
www.fs.fed.us/r9/forests/hiawatha/recreation/
lighthouses/peninsula_point/index.php

Point Aux Barques Lighthouse
Port Hope
www.pointeauxbarqueslighthouse.org

Point Betsie Lighthouse
Frankfort
(231) 352-7666
(231) 352-4915
www.pointbetsie.org

Point Iroquois Lighthouse / Hiawatha
National Forest
Brimley
(906) 635-5311
www.fs.fed.us/r9/forests/hiawatha/recreation/l
ighthouses/point_iroquois_light/
index.php

Rock Harbor Lighthouse / Isle Royale
National Park
Isle Royale
(906) 482-0984
www.nps.gov/isro

Sand Hills Lighthouse Inn
Ahmeek
(906) 337-1744
www.sandhillslighthouseinn.com

Sand Point Lighthouse / Ludington Park
Escanaba
(906) 789-6790
www.exploringthenorth.com/sandpoint/
light.html

Seul Choix Point Lighthouse
Gulliver
(906) 283-3183
www.greatlakelighthouse.com

South Manitou Island Lighthouse / Sleeping
Bear Dunes National Lakeshore
South Manitou Island
(231) 326-5134
www.nps.gov/slbe/planyourvisit/
smilighthouse.htm

St. Helena Island Light Station
St. Helena Island
(231) 436-5580 (Great Lakes Lighthouse
Keepers Association)
www.gllka.com/restoration/index.htm

Tawas Point Lighthouse / Tawas Point State
Park
East Tawas
(989) 362-5041
www.michigan.gov/hal/0,1607,7-160-
17447_18595_18614-67781—,00.html

White River Light Station
Whitehall
(231) 894-8265
www.whiteriverlightstation.org

MINNESOTA

Split Rock Lighthouse Historic Site / Split
Rock Lighthouse State Park
Two Harbors
(218) 226-6372
www.mnhs.org/places/sites/srl

Two Harbors Lighthouse / Lighthouse Bed &
Breakfast
Two Harbors
(218) 834-4814
www.lighthousebb.org

NEW HAMPSHIRE

Portsmouth Harbor Lighthouse
Portsmouth
www.lighthouse.cc/portsmouth

NEW JERSEY

Absecon Lighthouse
Atlantic City
(609) 449-1360
www.abseconlighthouse.org

Barnegat Lighthouse / Barnegat Lighthouse
State Park
Long Beach Island
(609) 494-2016
www.state.nj.us/dep/parksandforests/parks/
barnlig.html

Cape May Lighthouse
Cape May
(609) 884-5404
www.capemaymac.org

East Point Lighthouse
Heislerville
E-mail: eastpointlighthousenj@yahoo.com

Hereford Inlet Lighthouse
North Wildwood
(609) 522-4520
www.herefordlighthouse.org

Sandy Hook Lighthouse / Gateway National
Recreation Area
Highlands
(732) 872-5970
www.nps.gov/gate

Sea Girt Lighthouse
Sea Girt
(732) 974-0514
www.lonekeep.com/seagirtlighthouse

Twin Lights of Navesink / Twin Lights
Historic Site (one tower open)
Highlands
(732) 872-1814
www.twin-lights.org

NEW YORK

Bluff Point Lighthouse
Valcour Island
(518) 561-0340
www.clintoncountyhistorical.org/
lighthouse.html

The Charlotte-Genesee Lighthouse
Rochester
(585) 621-6179
www.geneseelighthouse.org

Dunkirk Lighthouse & Veterans Park
Museum
Dunkirk
(716) 366-5050
www.dunkirklighthouse.com

Fire Island Lighthouse / Fire Island National
Seashore
Fire Island
(631) 661-4876
www.fireislandlighthouse.com
www.nps.gov/fiis

Horton Point Lighthouse
Southold
(631) 765-5500
www.southoldhistoricalsociety.org/
lighthouse.htm

Jeffrey's Hook Lighthouse ("Little Red
Lighthouse") / Fort Washington Park
New York
(212) 304-2365
www.nycgovparks.org/sub_about/parks_
divisions/historic_houses/hh_little_red_
light.html

Montauk Point Lighthouse
Montauk
(631) 668-2544
www.montauklighthouse.com

Rondout Lighthouse / Hudson River
Maritime Museum
Kingston
(845) 338-0071
www.hrmm.org

Saugerties Lighthouse
Saugerties
(845) 247-0656
www.saugertieslighthouse.com

Sodus Bay Lighthouse & Museum
Sodus Point
(315) 483-4936
http://soduspointlighthouse.org

Stony Point Lighthouse / Stony Point
Battlefield State Historic Site
Stony Point
(845) 786-2521
http://nysparks.state.ny.us/sites/info.asp?
siteID=29

Tarrytown Lighthouse / Kingsland Point
Park
Village of Sleepy Hollow
(914) 366-5109
www.hudsonlights.com/tarrytown.htm

Thirty Mile Point Lighthouse / Golden Hill
State Park
Barker
(716) 795-3885
http://nysparks.state.ny.us/parks/info.asp?
parkID=111

Tibbets Point Lighthouse
Cape Vincent
(315) 654-2700
www.capevincent.org/lighthouse/
lighthouse_001.htm

NORTH CAROLINA

Baldhead Island Lighthouse (Old Baldy)
Baldhead Island
(910) 457-7481
www.oldbaldy.org

Cape Hatteras Lighthouse / Cape Hatteras
National Seashore
Buxton
(252) 995-4474
www.nps.gov/caha/lh.htm

Currituck Beach Lighthouse
Corolla
(252) 453-8152
www.currituckbeachlight.com

OHIO

Fairport Harbor Marine Museum and
Lighthouse
Fairport Harbor
(440) 354-4825
www.ncweb.com/org/fhlh

Lorain West Breakwater Lighthouse
Lorain
(440) 245-2563
www.lorainlighthouse.org

Marblehead Lighthouse / Marblehead
Lighthouse State Park
Marblehead
(419) 734-4424
www.dnr.ohio.gov/parks/parks/marble
head.htm

South Bass Island Lighthouse
South Bass Island
(419) 285-1800
http://ohioseagrant.osu.edu/stonelab/
workshops/?show=tours

OREGON

Cape Blanco Lighthouse / Cape Blanco
State Park / Bureau of Land Management
Point Orford
(541) 756-0100
www.oregonstateparks.org/park_62.php

Cape Meares Lighthouse / Cape Meares
State Scenic Viewpoint
Tillamook
(503) 842-3182
www.capemeareslighthouse.org

Heceta Head Lighthouse / Heceta Head
State Park
Yachats
(800) 551-6949 (state park)
(866) 547-3696 (interpretive center/inn)
www.oregonstateparks.org/park_124.php
www.hecetalighthouse.com

Umpqua River Lighthouse / Umpqua
Lighthouse State Park
Winchester Bay
(541) 271-4631
www.umpqualighthouse.org
www.oregonstateparks.org/park_121.php

Yaquina Bay Lighthouse (access to watch
room only)
Newport
(541) 265-5679
(541) 574-3129
www.yaquinalights.org

Yaquina Head Lighthouse / Yaquina Head
Outstanding Natural Area
Newport
(541) 574-3100
(541) 574-3129
www.yaquinalights.org

RHODE ISLAND

Block Island Southeast Lighthouse
Block Island
(401) 466-5009
http://lighthouse.cc/blockisoutheast/

Rose Island Lighthouse
Rose Island
(401) 847-4242
www.roseislandlighthouse.org

SOUTH CAROLINA

Hunting Island Lighthouse / Hunting Island
State Park
Hunting Island
(843) 838-2011
www.southcarolinaparks.com/park-finder/state-park/1019.aspx

TEXAS

Port Isabel Lighthouse State Historic Site
Port Isabel
(956) 943-2262
www.tpwd.state.tx.us/spdest/findadest/parks/
port_isabel_lighthouse

VIRGINIA

Assateague Lighthouse / Chincoteague
National Wildlife Refuge
Chincoteague
(757) 336-3696
www.assateagueisland.com/lighthouse/
lighthouse_info.htm
www.fws.gov/northeast/chinco

Cape Henry Lighthouse (Old)
Virginia Beach
(757) 422-9421
www.apva.org/capehenry
Note: New Cape Henry Light is at the same
site, but you can't climb it.

WASHINGTON

Admiralty Head Lighthouse / Fort Casey
State Park
Coupeville
(360) 678-4519
(360) 240-5584
www.admiraltyhead.wsu.edu

Alki Point Lighthouse
Seattle
(206) 217-6203

Gray's Harbor Lighthouse / Westport
Maritime Museum
Westport
(360) 268-0078
www.westportwa.com/museum

Lime Kiln Lighthouse / Lime Kiln Point
State Park
San Juan Island
(360) 378-2044
www.parks.wa.gov/parkpage.asp?selected-park=Lime%20Kiln%20Point

Mukilteo Light Station
Mukilteo
(425) 513-9602
http://mukilteohistorical.org

New Dungeness Light Station
Sequim
(360) 683-9166
www.newdungenesslighthouse.com

North Head Lighthouse / Cape
Disappointment State Park
Ilwaco
(360) 642-3078
www.parks.wa.gov/parkpage.asp?selectedpark
=Cape%+Disappointment

Point Robinson Lighthouse
Vashon Island
(206) 463-9602
www.vashonparkdistrict.org

WISCONSIN

Devils Island Light Tower / Apostle Islands
National Lakeshore
Devils Island
(715) 779-3397
www.nps.gov/apis

Eagle Bluff Lighthouse / Peninsula State
Park
Fish Creek
(920) 839-2377
www.eagleblufflighthouse.org

New Michigan Island Light Tower / Apostle
Islands National Lakeshore
Michigan Island
(715) 779-3397
www.nps.gov/apis

North Point Lighthouse / Lake Park
Milwaukee
(414) 332-6754
www.northpointlighthouse.org

Old Michigan Island Lighthouse / Apostle
Islands National Lakeshore
Michigan Island
(715) 779-3397
www.nps.gov/apis

Port Washington 1860 Light Station
Port Washington
(262) 284-7240
www.portlightstation.org

Potawatomie Lighthouse / Rock Island
State Park
Rock Island
(920) 847-2235
http://fori.us
www.dnr.state.wi.us/ORG/LAND/parks/
specific/rockisland

Raspberry Island Lighthouse / Apostle
Islands National Lakeshore
Raspberry Island
(715) 779-3397
www.nps.gov/apis

Sand Island Lighthouse / Apostle Islands
National Lakeshore
Sand Island
(715) 779-3397
www.nps.gov/apis

Southport Lighthouse and Keeper's Cottage
Kenosha, Wisconsin
(262) 654-5770
www.kenoshahistorycenter.org

Lighthouses with Museums and/or Access to Keeper's Quarters

(No tower access; in some cases you may be
able to enter base of lighthouse.)

Beavertail Lighthouse Museum
Jamestown, Rhode Island
(401) 423-3270
http://BeavertailLight.org

Block Island North Lighthouse
Block Island, Rhode Island
(401) 466-3213

Boca Grande Lighthouse Museum /
Gasparilla Island State Park
Gasparilla Island, Florida
(941) 964-0060
www.barrierislandparkssociety.org/
lighthouse.html

Cana Island Lighthouse / Door County
Maritime Museum
Cana Island, Wisconsin
(920) 743-5958
http://dcmm.org/canaisland.html

Colchester Reef Lighthouse / Shelburne
Museum
Shelburne, Vermont
(802) 985-3346
www.shelburnemuseum.org

Cook County Historical Society Museum
(Grand Marais Lighthouse)
Grand Marais, Minnesota
(218) 387-2883

Copper Harbor Lighthouse / Fort Wilkins
Historic State Park
Copper Harbor, Michigan
(906) 289-4215
www.sos.state.mi.us/history/museum/
musewil/chlight.html

Coquille River Lighthouse / Bullards Beach
State Park
Bandon, Oregon
(541) 347-2209
www.oregonstateparks.org/park_71.php

East Anacapa Visitors Center / Channel
Islands National Park (Anacapa Island
Lighthouse)
Channel Islands, California
(805) 658-5730
www.nps.gov/chis

Fenwick Island Lighthouse
Fenwick Island, Delaware
www.beach-net.com/lighthousefi.html

Keepers House Inn and Cottage (Robinson
Point Lighthouse)
Isle au Haut, Maine
(207) 460-0257
www.keepershouse.com

Lighthouse Keepers House and Museum
(Grand Marais Lighthouse)
Grand Marais, Michigan
(906) 494-2404
http://historicalsociety.grandmarais
michigan.com/#museumhoursofoperation

Marshall Point Lighthouse Museum
Port Clyde, Maine
(207) 372-6450
www.marshallpoint.org

Marquette Harbor Lighthouse
Marquette, Michigan
(906) 226-2006
http://mqtmaritimemuseum.com

Monhegan Museum (Monhegan Island
Lighthouse)
Monhegan Island, Maine
(207) 596-7003
www.monheganmuseum.org

Museum at Portland Head Light / Fort
Williams Park
Cape Elizabeth, Maine
(207) 799-2661
www.portlandheadlight.com

Pensacola Lighthouse
Pensacola, Florida
www.pensacolaauxiliary.com

Pigeon Point Lighthouse / Pigeon Point
Light Station State Historic Park
Pescadaro, California
(650) 879-2120
www.parks.ca.gov/default.asp?page_id=533

Point Bonita Lighthouse / Golden Gate
National Recreation Area
Sausalito, California
(415) 331-1540
www.nps.gov/goga/pobo.htm

Point Cabrillo Light Station and Preserve
Mendocino, California
(707) 937-6122
www.pointcabrillo.org

Point No Point Lighthouse and Park
Hansville, Washington
(360) 337-5350
www.kitsapgov.com/parks/regional
parks/point_no_point.htm

Point Pinos Lighthouse / Pacific Grove
Museum of Natural History
Pacific Grove, California
(831) 648-5716
www.pgmuseum.org

Point Reyes Lighthouse / Point Reyes
National Seashore
Point Reyes Station, California
(415) 669-1534
(415) 464-5100
www.nps.gov/pore/historyculture/people_
maritime_lighthouse.htm

Sturgeon Point Lighthouse and Museum
Harrisville, Michigan
www.theenchantedforest.com/Alcona
HistoricalSociety

Two Rivers North Pier Lighthouse / Historic
Rogers Street Fishing Village
Two Rivers, Wisconsin
(920) 793-5905
www.rogersstreet.com

Watch Hill Lighthouse Museum
Watch Hill, Rhode Island
www.rhodeislandlighthousehistory.info/
watch_hill_lighthouse.html

West Point Lighthouse / Discovery Park
Seattle, Washington
(206) 386-4236
www.ci.seattle.wa.us/parks/parkspaces/
discoverypark/lighthouse.htm

West Quoddy Head Lighthouse & Visitor
Center
Lubec, Maine
(207) 733-2180
www.westquoddy.com

Whitefish Point Light Station / Great Lakes
Shipwreck Museum
Paradise, Michigan
(906) 492-3747
www.shipwreckmuseum.com

Wood Island Lighthouse
Wood Island, Maine
www.woodislandlighthouse.org

Lightships

Ambrose
South Street Seaport Museum
New York, New York
(212) 748-8600
www.southstseaport.org

Chesapeake
Baltimore Maritime Museum
Baltimore, Maryland
(410) 396-3453
www.baltomaritimemuseum.org

Columbia
Columbia River Maritime Museum
Astoria, Oregon
(503) 325-2323
www.crmm.org

Huron
Port Huron Museum
Port Huron, Michigan
(810) 982-0891
www.phmuseum.org

Overfalls
Lewes, Delaware
www.overfalls.org

Portsmouth
Portsmouth Naval Shipyard Museum and
the Lightship Museum
Portsmouth, Virginia
(757) 393-8741
www.portsnavalmuseums.com

Relief
United States Lighthouse Society
Oakland, California
(415) 362-7255
(510) 272-0544
www.uslhs.org

Swiftsure
Northwest Seaport
Seattle, Washington
(206) 447-9800
www.nwseaport.org

Glossary

acetylene: Type of gas used to produce lights at some lighthouses before electricity. Early automated lighthouses relied on acetylene.

aeromarine beacon (aerobeacon): Weatherproof lights designed for airports; they replaced Fresnel lenses at some lighthouses.

aid to navigation: Any device not located on a vessel to help mariners; includes buoys, fog signals, and lighthouses.

Argand lamp: Oil lamp with a hollow circular wick and glass chimney that produced a brighter light than traditional oil lamps.

automated: Run by machine.

beacon: Device that helps guide mariners, including buoys, lighthouses, and signal fires.

bivalve lens (clamshell lens): Type of Fresnel lens shaped like an irregular oval. It has two bull's-eye lenses, one on either side.

breakwater light: Lighthouse or beacon placed at end of a long wall that protects harbors from high waves.

bull's-eye lens: The round magnifying lenses used in some Fresnel lens systems to create a flash.

buoy: Aid to navigation used to mark channels, harbors, shipwrecks, etc.

caisson: Foundation type popular for offshore lighthouses; name comes from use of a caisson, or tube, sunk to the bottom of the seabed.

catwalk: Raised walkway above a pier to help keepers reach a lighthouse when winds or waves are high; most common along the Great Lakes. Term is also used as a synonym for gallery.

cistern: Tank used for storing rainwater to be used for drinking and bathing water.

clockwork mechanism: Weight-driven system that had to be wound regularly; it was used to ring fog bells and rotate lighthouse lenses and reflectors before electricity.

Coast Guard, U.S.: Branch of the military now in charge of U.S. lighthouses.

crib: A foundation type used for offshore lighthouses with hard seabeds; most common along the Great Lakes.

daymark: Paint pattern or color on a lighthouse used to distinguish it from other lighthouses in the same region.

depot: Place where supplies for lighthouses were stored.

diaphone: Two-toned fog signal.

exposed screw pile: Foundation type that relied on oversized screws at tips of piles and disks placed above those screws to stabilize structure.

fixed light: A light from a lighthouse that remains on steadily, without flashing, at night or in bad weather.

flashing light: A type of light that exhibits a "flash" or period of light shorter in length than the period of darkness.

focal plane: The height above water of the beam from a lighthouse.

fog signal: A sound or electronic signal used to aid mariners when visibility is low.

Fresnel lens: Elaborate lens system using pieces of carefully cut glass to reflect and refract light into one powerful beam.

gallery: Deck(s) or balcony(ies) on a lighthouse that allow access outside.

Global Positioning System (GPS): A modern navigational system that relies on data transmitted by satellites.

hyper-radial (hyper-radiant) lens: Rare oversized Fresnel lens bigger than first-order lenses.

illuminant: Lamp oil, electricity, or other power source for lighthouse light.

incandescent oil vapor lamp: Lamp that produced a bright light by putting kerosene under intense pressure.

inspector: Government official that checked light stations to see if they were clean and in good working order.

isophase light: Light where duration of light and darkness are the same.

keeper: Person in charge of operating a lighthouse.

kerosene: Common fuel once used for oil lamps in U.S. lighthouses; sometimes referred to as mineral oil.

landfall light: Major seacoast light; the first thing mariners see when arriving near land.

lantern room (lantern): The enclosed area at the top of a lighthouse that houses its light.

Lewis lamp: Oil lamp invented by Winslow Lewis, who sold the patent for it to the U.S. government for use in lighthouses. Modeled after Argand lamp developed in Europe.

light list: Government publication that describes the appearance and location of a lighthouse and its light characteristic to help mariners pinpoint their positions.

lightship: Boat equipped with one or more lights that was used at offshore sites where a lighthouse could not be built; also known as a floating light, light-vessel, or light boat.

light station: The grounds surrounding a lighthouse, including the lighthouse and all related buildings (oil house, fog signal building, boat house, etc.).

LORAN: Short for long-range navigation; this electronic aid to navigation uses receivers to pick up signals from transmitting stations.

mercury bath (mercury float): A pool of mercury used to support heavy lenses, allowing them to revolve easily.

occulting light: Characteristic in which duration of light is longer than duration of darkness.

oil house: Small sturdy building where oil for lamps was stored.

order: Size and strength of Fresnel lens; first-order lenses were the largest and most powerful, except for hyper-radial lenses.

pharologist: A person who studies or is interested in lighthouses.

Pharos: First documented lighthouse in the world in Alexandria, Egypt; later used as a general term for a lighthouse.

pneumatic caisson: Foundation type where compressed air was used to create a working chamber inside a caisson at the bottom of the seabed.

Radio beacon: First electronic aid to navigation used in United States; replaced by radar and LORAN.

range lights: Pair of lights that guide mariners into harbors or channels. Rear range light is placed at higher elevation than front range light. When the lights line up, the mariner knows he is in the desired area for safe passage. Also called leading lights.

reflector: Shiny device placed behind light source to intensify beam.

screw pile: Foundation type with large screws at the end of each pile, or support, to anchor it in sand or soft soil.

sextant: Navigational instrument used to determine one's location using the position of the sun, moon, or stars.

skeletal lighthouse: Structure with enclosed lantern room and stairs, but no walls.

spark-plug light: Nickname for round lights on caisson foundations because they looked like automobile spark plugs.

stag station: Lighthouse where women and children were not allowed to live because of dangerous conditions.

straightpile: Foundation type that relied on straight piles, or supports, driven into rock or soil.

sun valve: Device that turned lighthouses powered by acetylene gas on and off automatically.

tender: Boat used to deliver construction materials or supplies to lighthouses.

Texas tower: Modern tower resembling an oil platform that includes a skeletal light and helicopter-landing pad.

twin lights: A pair of lights at the same site; used before flashing lights to help mariners distinguish one light station from others nearby.

watchroom: The room where the keeper stayed to watch the light during the night, it was usually located one level below the lantern room.

wave-swept tower: Tower with a solid base to provide stability against crashing waves.

whistle house: Fog signal building.

wickie: Nickname for lighthouse keeper, derived from era of lamps.

wrecker: Person who sold items salvaged from shipwrecks to earn a living; some wreckers, or "mooncussers," caused shipwrecks by shining lights along the coast to confuse sailors.

Selected Bibliography

Note: To see the sources of the quotes in this book, visit www.lighthousesforkids.com.

Books and Articles

Adamson, Hans Christian. *Keepers of the Lights: The Saga of Our Lighthouses, Lightships, and the Men Who Guide Those Who Sail the Seas.* New York: Greenberg Publishers, 1955.

Bachand, Robert G. *Northeast Lights: Lighthouses and Lightships Rhode Island to Cape May, N.J.* Norwalk, CT: Sea Sports Publications, 1989.

Bacon, Betty Byrnes. "Lighthouse Memories," compiled by Debra Ann Holmes. Brimley, MI: Bay Mills-Brimley Historical Research Society, 1989.

Browning, Robert Dr. "Lighthouse Evolution and Typology," Washington, D.C.: U.S. Coast Guard Historian's Office, n.d.

Cipra, David L. *Lighthouses, Lightships, and the Gulf of Mexico*. Alexandria, VA: Cypress Communications, 1997.

Clifford, Candace (project manager). *1994 Inventory of Historic Light Stations*. Washington, D.C.: Government Printing Office, 1994.

Clifford, Candace. *Nineteenth-Century Lights: Historic Images of American Lighthouses*. Alexandria, VA: Cypress Communications, 2000.

Clifford, Mary Louise, and J. Candace. *Women Who Kept the Lights: An Illustrated History of Female Lighthouse Keepers*. Williamsburg, VA: Cypress Communications, 1993.

De Wire, Elinor. *Guardians of the Lights: The Men and Women of the U.S. Lighthouse Service*. Sarasota, FL: Pineapple Press Inc., 1995.

De Wire, Elinor. *Lighthouses of the Pacific Coast: California, Oregon, Washington, Alaska, and Hawai'i*. St. Paul, MN: Voyageur Press, 2006.

D'Entremont, Jeremy. "Keeper Roscoe Chandler: Reliable and Resourceful." *Lighthouse Digest*, December 2002.

Engel, Norma. *Three Beams of Light*. San Diego: Tecolote Publications, 1986.

Furst, Glenn. *My Point of View* (n.p.), 1992.

Gibbs, Jim. *West Coast Lighthouses: A Pictorial History of the Guiding Lights of the Sea*. Seattle: Superior Publishing Co., 1974.

Gleason, Sarah C. *Kindly Lights: A History of the Lighthouses of Southern New England*. Boston: Beacon Press, 1991.

Great Lakes Lighthouse Keepers Association. *Instructions to Light-Keepers: A Photo Reproduction of the 1902 Edition of Instructions to Light-Keepers and Masters of Light-House Vessels*. Allen Park, MI: GLLKA, 1989.

Harrison, Tim, and Ray Jones. *Endangered Lighthouses: Stories and Images of America's Disappearing Lighthouses*. Guilford, CT: The Globe Pequot Press, 2001.

Historic Lighthouse Preservation Handbook. Washington, D.C.: U.S. Government Printing Office, 1997.

Holland, Francis Ross Jr. *America's Lighthouses: Their Illustrated History Since 1716*. Brattleboro, VT: The Stephen Greene Press, 1972.

Holland, F. Ross. *The Old Point Loma Lighthouse*. n.p.: Cabrillo Historical Association in cooperation with the National Park Service, 1978.

Holland, F. Ross Jr. *Great American Lighthouses*. Washington, D.C.: The Preservation Press, 1989.

Hyde, Charles K. *The Northern Lights: Lighthouses of the Upper Great Lakes*. 3rd ed. Lansing, MI: TwoPeninsula Press, 1990.

Jennings, Harold B. *A Lighthouse Family*. Orleans, MA: Lower Cape Publishing Co., 1989.

Jones, Ray, with *Lighthouse Digest* and the American Lighthouse Foundation. *The Lighthouse Encyclopedia: The Definitive Reference*. Guilford, CT: The Globe Pequot Press, 2004.

Menz, Katherine B. *Historic Furnishings Report: Point Loma Lighthouse*. Harpers Ferry, WV: National Park Service / U.S. Department of the Interior, 1978.

Nelson, Sharlene P., and Ted W. Nelson. *Umbrella Guide to Washington Lighthouses*. Friday Harbor, WA: Umbrella Books, 1990.

Noble, Dennis L. *Lighthouses & Keepers: The U.S. Lighthouse Service and Its Legacy*. Annapolis, MD: Naval Institute Press, 1997.

Owens, Cora Isabel. "Lighthouse Memories Part III (Point Arena)," *The Keeper's Log*, Fall 1989.

Roberts, Bruce, and Ray Jones. *American Lighthouses*. Old Saybrook, CT: The Globe Pequot Press, 1998.

Shelton-Roberts, Cheryl, and Bruce Roberts. *Lighthouse Families*. Birmingham, AL: Crane Hill Publishers, 1997.

Shultz, Denise. "Pharology 101—Mercury Float," *Lighthouses of Australia Inc. Monthly Bulletin*, May/June 2005.

Shanks, Ralph, and Lisa Woo Shanks (ed.). *Guardians of the Golden Gate: Lighthouses and Lifeboat Stations of San Francisco Bay*. Petaluma, CA: Costaño Books, 1990.

Stevenson, D. Alan. *The World's Lighthouses from Ancient Times to 1820*. Mineola, NY: Dover Publications Inc., 2002. Reprinted from Oxford University Press, 1959, *The World's Lighthouses Before 1820*.

Terras, Donald J. *The Grosse Point Lighthouse Evanston, Illinois: Landmark to Maritime History and Culture*. Evanston, IL: Windy City Press, 1995.

Titzell, Josiah. "Rachel Field: Portrait of a Troubadour," *The Horn Book Magazine*, November 1927.

Turbyville, Linda. *Bay Beacons: Lighthouses of the Chesapeake Bay*. Annapolis, MD: Eastwind Publishing, 1995.

Vojtech, Pat. *Lighting the Bay: Tales of Chesapeake Lighthouses*. Centerville, MD: Tidewater Publishers, 1996.

Ward, Jane. "Hooper Strait Lighthouse, rev. ed." Watertown, NY: privately printed, 1995.

Wass, Philmore B. *A Lighthouse in My Life: The Story of a Maine Lightkeeper's Family*. Camden, ME: Down East Books, 1987.

Weiss, George. *The Lighthouse Service: Its History, Activities and Organization*. Baltimore: The Johns Hopkins Press, 1926.

Williams, Peter. *Beacon on the Rock: The Dramatic History of Lighthouses from Ancient Greece to the Present Day*. New York: Barron's Education Series Inc., 2001.

Yocum, Thomas, Bruce Roberts, and Cheryl Shelton-Roberts. *Cape Hatteras: America's Lighthouse*. Nashville, TN: Cumberland House, 1999.

Videos

Brzozowski, Richard. *Keepers of the Light*. Allen Park, MI: Great Lakes Lighthouse Keepers Association.

Duffus, Kevin, and Susan Kavanaugh. *Move of the Century: Cape Hatteras Light*. Raleigh, NC: Video Marketing Group Inc., 1999.

Grant, Jon. *Staying at a Lighthouse: A Legendary Lighthouses Special*. Burke, VA: Driftwood Productions Inc., 1998.

Other Sources

In addition, I consulted several articles from the following publications: *The Beacon*, published by the Great Lakes Lighthouse Keepers Association, Mackinaw City, Michigan; *Lighthouse Digest*, Wells, Maine; *The Keeper's Log*, published by the U.S. Lighthouse Society, San Francisco; the *Lighthouse Service Bulletin*, published by the U.S. government from 1912 to 1939, and various copies of the *Light-House Board* annual reports.

Index